Ending Poverty: Jobs, Not Welfare

Hyman P. Minsky

Levy Economics Institute
Annandale-on-Hudson, N.Y.

The Levy Economics Institute of Bard College, founded in 1986 through the generous support of Bard College Trustee Leon Levy (1925–2003), is a nonprofit, nonpartisan, public policy research organization. The Institute is independent of any political or other affiliation, and encourages diversity of opinion in the examination of economic policy issues.

The purpose of the Institute's research and activities is to enable scholars and leaders in business, labor, and government to work together on problems of common interest. Its findings are disseminated—via publications, conferences, seminars, congressional testimony, and partnerships with other nonprofits—to a global audience of public officials, private sector executives, academics, and the general public. Through this process of scholarship, analysis, and informed debate, the Institute generates effective public policy responses to economic problems that profoundly influence the quality of life in the United States and abroad.

ISBN 978-1-936192-31-1
©2013 Levy Economics Institute of Bard College. All rights reserved.

Front Cover: Achille Beltrame, illustration of unemployed workers rallying in New York City, *La Domenica del Corriere*, 1930.
©De Agostini Picture Library/A. Dagli Orti/The Bridgeman Art Library

Back Cover: Hyman P. Minsky, Cambridge, Massachusetts, 1948.
Photo: Anne Tolstoi Wallach

Contents

Acknowledgments i

Preface
Dimitri B. Papadimitriou iii

Introduction
L. Randall Wray xi

1. The Role of Employment Policy (1965) 1

2. Effects of Shifts of Aggregate Demand upon
   Income Distribution (1968) 27

3. Policy and Poverty (1969) 43

4. The Macroeconomics of a Negative Income Tax (1969) 81

5. Where the American Economy—and Economists—
   Went Wrong (1972) 103

6. The Poverty of Economic Policy (1975) 125

7. Full Employment and Economic Growth as an Objective
   of Economic Policy: Some Thoughts on the Limits of
   Capitalism (1994) 157

Index 183

Biographies 187

Acknowledgments

This book would not have been possible without the continued guidance and support of Leonardo Burlamaqui of the Ford Foundation. It was Leonardo's insight to push for the publication of Hyman Minsky's work on the relationship of poverty and full employment—a vital theme in Minsky's writing that deserves to be as widely acknowledged as his work on financial instability.

Special thanks to the teams at the Levy Economics Institute and the Bard College Publications Office for their assistance in putting this book together, and to Andrew Sheng for his financial support for the digitization of the Minsky Archive.

Research by Stephanie Kelton, with archival assistance from Éric Tymoigne, helped furnish the material adapted for the introduction to this volume.

Dimitri B. Papadimitriou, L. Randall Wray, and Jan Kregel
Annandale-on-Hudson, N.Y.

Preface

Dimitri B. Papadimitriou

When the recent financial crash shook the global economy—and with it some of the key assumptions underlying a great deal of orthodox economic theory—many turned to the late Hyman P. Minsky's writing on financial instability for answers. Now, as financial institutions return to business as usual and the lingering damage to the real economy draws our attention to the struggles of the unemployed, the working poor, and all those who have been left behind by the latest phase of finance-dominated capitalism, another aspect of Minsky's work needs to be injected into the conversation.

Minsky concerned himself as much with the issues of poverty and full employment as he did with financial fragility, and just as his work on financial restructuring and reregulation provides an essential guide for thinking about the limitations of our current approach to financial reform, his writing on poverty and employment can shed light on the enduring failure of conventional public policy with respect to the problem of poverty. In the interests of such illumination, the present volume gathers together a selection of Minsky's published and unpublished work, spanning roughly three decades, on poverty and the challenge and promise of full employment.

Most of the papers and manuscripts assembled here were written in the 1960s and early 1970s against the backdrop of the War on Poverty. These early writings are not, however, of purely historical interest. Although most of the papers are 40-plus years old, they hold up well. If anything, they are even more relevant today, as the unemployment rate has trended upward, income has become more unequal, and chronic long-term unemployment has become an even bigger problem.

In the introduction to this volume, L. Randall Wray frames Minsky's approach to poverty in the context of the latter's critique of the policy strategies pursued in the Kennedy–Johnson War on Poverty and of the economic theories that underlay those strategies. The astute reader will notice, however, that the present-day menu of policy options, and the intellectual framework that supports those conventional options (and forecloses alternatives), has changed little since 1965, when Minsky wrote "The Role of Employment Policy," which forms the first chapter in this collection. The difference today, perhaps, is that poverty has been relegated to the backwoods of the US policy landscape. When the issue does come up, however, the conversation does not often stray very far from the standard prescriptions of growth, transfers, and training: a cocktail that, in Minsky's view, would be just as ineffective today as it was half a century ago.

Retraining and "upgrading" workers without ensuring that there are enough jobs to go around is akin, as Minsky puts it in chapter 1, "to the great error-producing sin of infielders—throwing the ball before you have it." The missing ingredient in the War on Poverty, and in today's policy strategies, is a commitment to what Minsky called "tight full employment," which he associated with an unemployment rate as low as 2.5 percent.

In an unfinished working paper from 1994, Minsky and I wrote that the free market system as it existed at the time could not guarantee that a close approximation to full employment would be the "normal condition" of the economy (Papadimitriou and Minsky 1994). Nothing has happened in the last decade to change that verdict. Private markets, left to their own devices, are not going to get us to sustained full employment—let alone the 2.5 percent unemployment rate that Minsky regarded as central to a meaningful antipoverty campaign. Public action is essential.

The key to sustained, tight full employment, in Minsky's view, is direct job creation. In sketching out his preferred policy framework, he turned to the model offered by the public employment programs of the New Deal: the Works Progress Administration (WPA), Civilian Conservation Corps (CCC), and National Youth Administration (NYA). Minsky and I noted the irony that the New Deal, which emphasized the virtue of work and employment, ended up surviving largely in the form of transfer payment schemes such as Social Security (Papadimitriou and Minsky 1994). Reaching tight full employment would require a return to the forgotten side of the New Deal model: the creation and expansion of modern equivalents of the WPA/CCC/NYA trio of work-based programs.

Preface

In Minsky's updated version, the government would step forward as an "employer of last resort" (ELR) by offering a job at a minimum wage to anyone willing and able to work. The ELR proposal is fleshed out in various ways throughout the papers collected here, and more recent work inspired by Minsky's ELR has taken the basic idea in further directions, including jobs programs that are administered through the nonprofit and social entrepreneurial sectors (Tcherneva 2012) and programs that focus on the delivery of social care services (Antonopoulos 2007). But one of the enduring principles that underlies these various ELR or ELR-inspired schemes is a recognition of the role of income from work as a supporting pillar of individual dignity. And although the implementation of an ELR program would help alleviate periodic deep unemployment crises like the one the US economy is currently limping through, Minsky also envisaged the ELR as a tool for making full employment a permanent feature of the economy. As we wrote in 1994,

> There is a need for permanent instruments of policy which generate an infinitely elastic demand for work that is useful. The desirable situation is that at every moment in time the number of unfilled jobs is greater than the number of unemployed. This can only be guaranteed if the government acts as an employer who has a vast amount of projects that need to be done and is willing and able to pay to get those jobs done.

Without direct job creation programs underpinning a commitment to full employment, many conventional policy tools, on their own, are going to be inadequate to the challenge of alleviating poverty. As Minsky explains in chapter 2, standard aggregate demand stimulus through tax cuts and spurs to private investment will generate inflation and financial instability well before they secure anything resembling tight full employment. And while he recognized that a successful antipoverty campaign ultimately requires dealing with income distribution, in chapter 3 Minsky articulates a set of economic barriers to approaching the poverty problem via a more equitable distribution of the gains from economic growth, dwelling in particular on the danger of inflation. Minsky explains how direct job creation programs along the lines of an ELR would help overcome some of these obstacles. In addition to creating income-earning opportunities for the unemployed, tight full employment through direct job creation would create conditions in which low wages would rise faster than high wages. In this chapter, Minsky also reveals his sensitivity to the challenge of shaping an antipoverty strategy that can draw broad popular support. He argues that ELR-style service programs are more likely to build public legitimacy, as compared to a purely transfer-based approach, to the extent that they are regarded as yielding recognized benefits, in the form of goods and services, to the broader population.

In chapter 4, Minsky analyzes the likely macroeconomic effects of a proposed "negative income tax," a policy that drew some high-profile support in the 1970s and that bears a family resemblance to the currently in-vogue idea of basic income grants. He cautions that a negative income tax and other "social dividend" schemes harbor inflationary dangers, such that the real value of program recipients' benefits can "inflate out," leaving the poor and those with modest incomes not much better off.

Minsky's objections to the War on Poverty were not simply over matters of policy detail. As noted, they were also objections to the fundamental theoretical assumptions that motivated this failed approach. In chapter 5, Minsky tackles what he regarded as one of the chief theoretical barriers to reorienting the economy around full employment: the "neoclassical synthesis."

In chapter 6, Minsky folds his account of financial fragility and instability into the discussion of poverty and full employment, and takes on what he calls the "welfare mess." Minsky was not an opponent of the welfare state, but he saw it as radically incomplete in the absence of a commitment to full employment. Transfer programs such as food stamps are partly a measure of the compassion of a society, of our "national conscience and affection for man," as he puts it; but as a standalone poverty-alleviation strategy, they must fail. What is needed in place of a strictly "transfer-based" approach to poverty, says Minsky, is a "job-based" strategy.

Preface

Although his account of the evolution of the economy toward financial instability and his work on restructuring the financial system have recently received more attention than his writing on full employment, for Minsky these topics are intimately connected. This is evident throughout most of the chapters in this volume, and in chapter 7, originally published in 1994, Minsky draws out the connections even more explicitly. Here he identifies and elaborates on two fundamental flaws of capitalism: a failure to reach and sustain full employment, and a financial system that tends toward debt deflation dynamics leading to deep depressions. The American economy is a capitalist economy with a complex financial system, in which financial contracts are exchanges of money "now" for money "later." The tendency of the system to generate financial crises, Minsky asserts in chapter 7, "cannot be eradicated from any form of market capitalism in which liabilities exist that are prior commitments of the gross nominal profit flows of businesses." New Deal–era financial reforms helped mitigate the problem by constraining the use of excessive debts for specified purposes, and the resulting regulatory structure formed part of the new model of capitalism that successfully delivered prosperity and stability for decades to follow, but the underlying flaw did not disappear. By the 1980s, according to Minsky, the financial system had evolved and deregulation had proceeded to the point that a newly fragile financial system had developed. The financial system was reconstituted in the 1930s; an "overhaul of capitalism," he writes in the last chapter, is once again needed.

In this final chapter, Minsky writes about the challenges faced by the Clinton administration, but one could easily substitute "Obama" for "Clinton" and the message would still resonate. In fact, this chapter is even more relevant today, since we have now experienced the massive debt deflation that Minsky describes here. In the end, we did not get a "new, new model of capitalism" from the Clinton administration along the lines recommended by Minsky (the Gramm-Leach-Bliley Act of 1999 represented quite the opposite), and so far, despite the passage of the 2010 Dodd-Frank Act, we have yet to see it from the Obama administration either (see LEI 2012).

The current phase of capitalism still needs an overhaul, a return to the broad model, not necessarily the specifics, of the New Deal. That means financial reregulation, to promote stability and ensure that the financial sector serves as a handmaiden to the capital development of the economy, creating a vibrant and stable private sector; and direct job creation programs, to ensure the tight full employment that is crucial to battling poverty and the large-scale waste of human potential.

Public discussion of poverty has become muted in the United States, and although we may no longer be fighting a declared war against poverty, the problem has by no means disappeared. In today's economy, the gains from economic growth flow even more unequally to the top tier of the income distribution, and policymakers have not only failed to offer a plausible path back to full employment in the wake of the financial crisis, but they also appear willing to declare victory and go home with an unemployment rate just barely below 8 percent. This is the true measure of the failure of the current iteration of American capitalism: chronic and systemic unemployment that relegates all too many to the scrap heap of the economy (Papadimitriou and Minsky 1994).

"To meet the problems of an economic crisis," Minsky writes, "it is necessary to search out new directions in economic theory" (chapter 5, 105). We hope that Minsky's work aids in this search for new directions and helps sweep aside some of the theoretical detritus that stands in the way of policies that can deliver more broad-based prosperity.

Sources

Antonopoulos, R. 2007. "The *Right* to a Job, the *Right Types* of Projects: Employment Guarantee Policies from a Gender Perspective." Working Paper No. 516. Annandale-on-Hudson, N.Y.: Levy Economics Institute. September.

LEI (Levy Economics Institute). 2012. *Beyond the Minsky Moment: Where We've Been, Why We Can't Go Back, and the Road Ahead for Financial Reform.* Annandale-on-Hudson, N.Y.: Levy Economics Institute.

Papadimitriou, D. B., and H. P. Minsky. 1994. "Why Not Give Full Employment a Chance?" Paper 173. Hyman P. Minsky Archive, Levy Economics Institute, Annandale-on-Hudson, N.Y.

Tcherneva, P. R. 2012. "Full Employment through Social Entrepreneurship: The Nonprofit Model for Implementing a Job Guarantee." Policy Note 2012/2. Annandale-on-Hudson, N.Y.: Levy Economics Institute. March.

Introduction

L. Randall Wray

The War on Poverty is a war most Americans would like to forget, a war only halfheartedly embraced by Washington, a war decisively lost. Hyman Minsky characterized the original War on Poverty as an attempt to "upgrade workers," and numerous programs have been created since 1964 to improve the education, skills, and incentives of the jobless to make them more appealing to private sector employers. Further, "Keynesian" policies to raise aggregate demand in order to stimulate private sector employment have also been adopted in the postwar period in the belief that economic growth would raise the demand for labor and thereby "lift the boats" of the poor. Still, unemployment rates have trended upward, long-term unemployment has become increasingly concentrated among the labor force's disadvantaged, real wages for most workers have declined, and poverty rates have remained stubbornly high.

The economic theories on which the War on Poverty was based misunderstand the nature of poverty. The notion that economic growth, together with supply-side policies to upgrade workers and provide proper work incentives, would be enough to eliminate poverty was recognized by Minsky at the time to be fallacious. According to Minsky, the critical component that was missing in 1964, and that remains AWOL to this day, is a government commitment to full employment. Only a targeted jobs program paying decent wages will successfully fight poverty among the nonaged in a politically acceptable manner.

Johnson Declares War: The Economic Opportunity Act

In his first State of the Union address on January 8, 1964, President Lyndon B. Johnson declared an "unconditional war on poverty," and the Economic Opportunity Act was submitted to Congress later that year. According to Johnson, the plan was designed to deal with the causes of poverty, rather than simply to try to ameliorate its

---

* This introduction draws on Bell and Wray (2004).

consequences. By expanding educational and training opportunities for the poor, Johnson believed it would be possible to end poverty forever. While the act established the Head Start program to provide preschool education as well as some job training and funds for the unemployed, it did not contain any significant job-creation programs. Johnson considered the Economic Opportunity Act "a total commitment . . . to pursue victory over the most ancient of mankind's enemies" (Public Papers of the Presidents, 380). It hardly seems controversial to suggest that nearly five decades later, the enemy is still at large.

The CEA and President Kennedy

It is perhaps not sufficiently recognized that the War on Poverty got its start under President Kennedy, whose Council of Economic Advisers (CEA) played a significant role in shaping the strategy that would be pursued. The key program omission from the War on Poverty was direct job creation. This resulted from the CEA's belief that (1) poverty was not inextricably linked to unemployment, (2) unemployment could in any case be sufficiently reduced through aggregate fiscal policies (such as Kennedy's tax cut of 1963), and (3) millions of Americans would have to be maintained as an unemployed buffer stock to keep inflation in check. These views still hold sway among economists.

The CEA was able to turn the president and policy against the dominant "structuralist" views of unemployment held by many economists, most policymakers, and even most of Congress—and by Kennedy's close adviser, John Kenneth Galbraith—all of whom believed that unemployment above 2 percent was unacceptable. The structuralists argued that demand stimulus alone could never generate jobs where they were most needed—for low-skilled workers, and for African Americans. Further, given that the CEA was prepared to accept 4 percent (or more) unemployment as "full employment," and as African American unemployment rates ran two to three times higher than the overall unemployment rates, a War on Poverty formulated by the CEA could never have made much of a dent in African American poverty.

Introduction

After Kennedy's assassination, it was left to Johnson to carry the War on Poverty through Congress. Judith Russell (2004) builds a convincing case that the mood of the country and of Congress was such that a massive job creation program sold by a president with Johnson's political acumen would have garnered sufficient support. It was the right idea at the ideal time, with a brief window of opportunity to put in place a jobs program that had a real chance at eliminating most poverty. It was the CEA's version of Keynesianism—based on "priming the pump" to raise demand—that played the major role in closing that window. It convinced the president that a jobs program was not a necessary element in the fight against poverty. Another culprit was the widespread belief that the poor had to be changed before poverty could be eliminated, based on the "culture of poverty" theses associated most closely with Daniel Patrick Moynihan.

The War on Poverty: Minsky's Assessment

Minsky considered the War on Poverty "a conservative rebuttal to an ancient challenge of the radicals, that capitalism necessarily generates 'poverty in the midst of plenty'" (chapter 1, 1). As he saw it, Johnson's version of this "conservative rebuttal" was fundamentally flawed. Instead of providing the impoverished with an opportunity to work, it provided them with the opportunity to learn *how* to work.

Minsky blamed a great deal of American poverty on unemployment. And, since he blamed unemployment on our economic system rather than on the shortcomings of its workers, he rejected supply-side "solutions" such as workfare, training, education, and so-called "incentives to work." But he also rejected the kind of demand stimulus policies that have been called upon to stimulate employment since World War II. In 1975, a decade into the War on Poverty, he argued: "We have to reverse the thrust of policy of the past 40 years and move towards a system in which labor force attachment is encouraged. But to do that we must make jobs available; any policy strategy which does not take job creation as its first and primary objective is but a continuation of the impoverishing strategy of the past decade" (chapter 6, 141). Since the postwar antipoverty strategy had proven ineffectual, Minsky believed that policymakers should return to the kind of strategy that characterized policymaking prior to World War II—namely programs to provide public employment.

One could see the War on Poverty as a victory for the "Age of Keynes" but a defeat for a real antipoverty strategy, in the sense that it brought with it a belief in the importance of maintaining aggregate demand in order to promote economic growth but neglected the importance of jobs in reducing poverty. There was an alternative Keynesian view to which Kennedy and Johnson could have turned for support of a real antipoverty program.

A Structuralist Interpretation of Relationships among Employment, Unemployment, and Poverty

Structuralists tended to emphasize job mismatch: even at cyclical peaks when the aggregate number of jobs might be sufficient, the skills, education, and other characteristics of a substantial set of the unemployed would leave them without jobs. Such views were dominant among policymakers of the early 1960s (Russell 2004). Similar views were also favored at the end of the 1990s as the "New Economy" boom left low-skilled workers behind (Pigeon and Wray 2000). But the structuralists of the early 1960s went further, because they argued that technological and other structural changes to job markets would outstrip any ability to educate and retrain displaced workers. In other words, they were highly skeptical that supply-side policies alone would be sufficient to resolve the growing unemployment problem. What was needed was a combination of "active labor market" policies and direct job-creation programs for the structurally displaced.

Minsky pointed out that even if the economy were not dynamically creating structurally displaced workers, labor market supply-side programs would have little effect for up to 20 years—the "gestation" period required to produce a worker: "We are learning that what happens to a child between the ages of three to five is of vital importance in determining the capabilities of the adult. Thus, preschool training is necessary to break the vicious circle of poverty. But if this view is true, then it takes 18 to 20 years to realize the benefits from such programs" (chapter 1, 20). In a dynamic society that is always moving, and generally raising, the skills goalposts, that long gestation period almost guarantees that many individuals achieving the age of labor force entry will not be prepared for the jobs that then exist. Thus, there would always be a mismatch between labor "supply" and "demand."

As a student of the institutionalist tradition at the University of Chicago, Minsky was undoubtedly aware of the institutionalist approach to labor markets: the structuralist approach. He emphasized that joblessness, insufficient hours of work, and low pay combined to create poverty among the able-bodied. He was willing to grant that a system of welfare would be required to deal with those who could not, or should not, work. He insisted, however, that a comprehensive jobs program together with an effective and adequate minimum wage would go a long way toward eliminating poverty among those willing and able to work. Significantly, he called for a "tight full employment" goal of 2.5 percent unemployment.

Compared with the expected 5.2 percent unemployment rate in 1965, he calculated this would have increased GNP by $34 billion to $53 billion (using Okun's law, according to which each one percentage point reduction of unemployment raises GNP by 3 percent). Minsky pointed out that this is far above the estimated $11 billion or $12 billion it would take to raise the incomes of all those living in poverty above the poverty line for that year. Hence, while a comprehensive employment strategy might not resolve all poverty problems, it would certainly generate more than enough GNP to eliminate poverty, provided that the GNP gains were appropriately distributed.

The Strategy of Growth through Private Investment

As mentioned, the CEA pushed the notion of pump-priming to generate growth. In the postwar era, with the exception of defense spending, "the preferred instrument for generating expansion has been a tax cut or loophole, i.e., the shifting of command over resources to private hands" (chapter 5, 112). These "Keynesian" policies to promote full employment relied on a favorable business environment to stimulate investment spending. Various tax incentives, including accelerated depreciation and investment tax credits, were a common feature of the postwar investment strategy (Tobin 1966). Policymakers also tried to increase the certainty of capital income through the use of government contracts with guaranteed profits, such as those granted to the defense, transportation, and housing industries.

However, Minsky (1973) argued that there were four problems with the high-investment strategy. First, tax incentives to shift income to capital exacerbate inequality between ordinary workers and those who have money to invest. Second, high capital incomes would lead to opulent consumption by the rich and emulative consumption by the less affluent, creating the potential for demand-pull inflation. Third, contracts granted to sophisticated, high-tech industries generate demand for skilled, high-wage labor, thereby exacerbating income inequality within the labor force. Finally, by targeting the size and surety of capital income, tax-cut programs would increase business confidence and debt financing, and borrowers' margins of safety would decline. Thus, a private investment strategy can lead to a debt-financed investment boom, thereby undermining the stability of the financial system.[1]

In sum, the postwar era was characterized by a preference for private investment strategies. Even as the War on Poverty got under way, the Johnson administration demonstrated its preference for private sector spending strategies, passing tax cuts in 1964 and again in 1965 and 1966. By encouraging private sector spending (especially investment), policymakers aimed to stimulate growth in total income. But these strategies did little to improve the conditions of lower-middle-income workers (e.g., factory workers), whose real incomes declined by 2.5 percent over the period 1965–70 (chapter 5, 114). Worse, the private investment strategies tended to exacerbate income inequality, generate inflation, and undermine financial stability.

Public Employment Strategy

Even though the Kennedy and Johnson administrations succeeded in generating a postwar boom that reduced unemployment rates, policymakers failed to understand that "policy weapons which are sufficient to move an economy from slack to sustained full employment are not sufficient to sustain full employment" (chapter 5, 122). As long as policymakers continued to favor private investment strategies, there would be no sustained strides made in the war against poverty from one business cycle to the next.[2] Minsky's alternative would stress high consumption fueled by policies that would increase wages and incomes at the bottom of the distribution. Further, government spending should play a major role in generating growth. Hence, Minsky's policies would favor both greater equality and greater stability. This ties together Minsky's two research agendas: financial stability on the one hand, and full employment with greater equality on the other.

To improve the lot of the poor permanently, Minsky believed that policymakers needed to address the question of income distribution, and that the most effective way to do so would be through the promotion and maintenance of full employment. By this, Minsky meant that it was necessary to achieve and sustain "tight full employment,"[3] which he defined as the situation that "exists when over a broad cross-section of occupations, industries, and locations, employers, at going wages and salaries, would prefer to employ more workers than they in fact do" (chapter 1, 3).

In order to reach this goal sustainably, Minsky advocated that government become an employer of last resort (ELR). The ELR proposal, which has been taken up by a number of analysts (Wray 1997, Papadimitriou 1999, Antonopoulos 2007), calls upon the federal government to institute a job assurance program similar to the New Deal's Works Progress Administration (WPA), Civilian Conservation Corps (CCC), and National Youth Administration (NYA) programs. The federal government would fund a job guarantee program, setting the price of (unskilled) labor and adjusting the number of jobs to the number in need of work.[4]

Minsky saw clear advantages to this program. First, he expected it to eliminate the kind of poverty resulting solely from joblessness. Whereas the investment strategy begins with demand increases for specialized labor, hoping for the trickle-down creation of low-skilled jobs, the employment strategy "takes the unemployed as they are and tailor-makes jobs to their skills" (Minsky 1972b, 6). Second, if the existence of tight labor markets draws additional workers into the labor force, the number of workers per family will increase, moving some families who are in or near poverty away from it. Third, a tight labor market strategy should improve the distribution of income among workers, as market processes raise the wages of low-income workers faster than the wages of high-income workers.[5] Fourth, by discontinuing the preferential treatment of capital income, Minsky believed that it was possible to "decrease [labor–profit] inequality by decreasing capital's share of income" (Minsky 1973, 94). Fifth, Minsky believed that by deemphasizing investment-led growth, the likelihood of financial fragility would decrease. Finally, a public employment strategy frees policymakers from the overriding need to induce investment through tax incentives.

Barriers to Attaining and Sustaining Tight Full Employment

Minsky seemed to anticipate the kinds of "pie in the sky" objections that might be raised, but he recognized that legitimate barriers must be taken into account: "Economic forces can frustrate programs if either the policy objective is inconsistent with such forces or if the program is so poorly conceived that it quite unnecessarily runs afoul of a barrier, even though the objective is, in principle, attainable" (chapter 3, 45).

One such frustrating force is inflation. "The policy problem," he argued, is to achieve and sustain tight full employment "without an inflationary rise in prices and wages" (Minsky 1972b, 5). But Minsky's antipoverty campaign called for "a rapid increase of those wages that are close to or below the poverty line" (chapter 1, 9). He recognized that there might be an inflationary bias in a policy of this sort, particularly if the productivity (output per hour) of the low-wage workers failed to keep pace with their wage increases.

In order to keep the overall price level fairly stable, prices of other goods and services would have to be constrained. Minsky suggested that in the high-wage industries, wages "would have to rise by less than the increases in the productivity of their workers"; to prevent firms from simply increasing their profits, it was necessary to ensure that "management in these often oligopolistic industries would have to pass this decline in unit costs on to their customers" (chapter 1, 9). Thus, he argued that "effective profit and price constraints would have to accompany tight full employment" (Minsky 1972b, 6).[6] If inflationary pressures were not contained, Minsky feared that the "political popularity of full employment" would be undermined (chapter 3, 69).

The inflation constraint is, however, much less of a concern in today's global economy. First, the deflationary pressures around the globe are substantial as many nations keep domestic demand depressed in order to run trade surpluses, looking to the United States to provide demand for the world's "excess" output. This means that US firms face substantial price competition so that even relatively rapid growth, such as that experienced in the Clinton expansion, does not produce inflationary pressures. Second, removal of trade restrictions together with technological advances has increased wage competition from abroad, especially from India and China, reducing the likelihood that low unemployment could generate a wage-price spiral.

The final institutional barrier concerns the exchange rate regime. Most of Minsky's papers on antipoverty policy were written in the 1960s or early 1970s, when US policy was constrained by an international monetary system with fixed exchange rates. Because the integrity of the Bretton Woods system rested on dollar convertibility to gold, policymakers had to restrict their fiscal and monetary operations to those that would not adversely affect the balance of payments. In Minsky's words:

> To a considerable extent, ever since 1958 the needs of the dollar standard have acted as a constraint upon domestic income. We have not had tight labor markets because of the peculiar bind that the dollar is in internationally.

> It is apparently appropriate to allude to William Jennings Bryan by saying that, in part, the cross that the American poor bear is made of gold. . . . The solution to the gold standard barrier is simple: get rid of the gold standard (chapter 1, 18).

Today the dollar is a floating currency, so that policy is not constrained by the need to protect foreign reserves. Thus, the primary barrier to attaining and sustaining tight full employment is political will.[7]

Conclusion

Private investment strategies together with policies to "improve" the characteristics of poor people have dominated the postwar approach to poverty. And, while the 1950s and 1960s are commonly referred to as the "Golden Age" of US capitalism, important barriers prevented the American economy from sustaining what Minsky characterized as tight full employment.

Minsky's fundamental argument is simple: (1) poverty is largely an employment problem; (2) tight full employment improves incomes at the bottom of the wage spectrum; and (3) a program of direct job creation is necessary to sustain tight full employment. Thus, he argued that a program of direct job creation was a "necessary ingredient of any war against poverty" (chapter 1, 1). As Minsky puts it: "The New Deal, with its WPA, NYA, and CCC, took workers as they were and generated jobs for them. . . . The resurrection of WPA and allied projects should be a major weapon of the War on Poverty" (chapter 1, 20).

Unfortunately, Johnson's Economic Opportunity Act did not provide for significant job creation. Instead, the War on Poverty aimed to improve the skills and knowledge of the impoverished, hoping to "end poverty forever" by offering education and training to those living in or near poverty. Almost five decades later, we are still pursuing the same failed policies. Minsky teaches us that until we change tactics, until we commit to full employment, we will continue to lose the war against poverty.

Introduction

Notes

1. For more on this connection to financial instability, see Minsky (1986).
2. While overall poverty rates did decline after 1965, the gains were concentrated only among the elderly. This was due to Social Security benefit payments, not due to the War on Poverty. See Bell and Wray (2004).
3. Minsky used, as an interim measure of tight full employment, an official rate of unemployment of 3.0 percent. He considered this a modest target, given that measured rates in Europe had been much lower than 3.0 percent. But he also viewed it as a desirable objective, since it was significantly better than anything the United States had achieved since 1953 (see chapter 2).
4. The details of an ELR program can get quite complex (e.g., the inclusion of health benefits, child care, pensions, and so on). For more on the intricacies of the proposal, readers should consult Wray (1998). For my purposes, it is sufficient to note that such a program may be administered locally (indeed, this is probably preferable), but it must be funded federally.
5. Here, Minsky refers to a study published in the *Quarterly Journal of Economics* (Anderson 1964), which showed a narrowing of wage differentials during periods of extreme labor-market tightness. James K. Galbraith (2000) has focused on the same patterns.
6. Minsky also proposed the elimination of taxes on corporate income and corporate contributions to Social Security, both of which he considered inflationary (Hawley 1981, 10).
7. Wray (1998) demonstrates how Minsky's employer-of-last-resort program could be implemented in a noninflationary way.

Sources

Anderson, W. H. L. 1964. "Trickling Down: The Relationship between Economic Growth and the Extent of Poverty among American Families." *Quarterly Journal of Economics* 78(4): 511–24.

Antonopoulos, R. 2007. "The *Right* to a Job, the *Right Types* of Projects: Employment Guarantee Policies from a Gender Perspective." Working Paper No. 516. Annandale-on-Hudson, N.Y.: Levy Economics Institute. September.

Bell, S. A., and L. R. Wray. 2004. "The War on Poverty after 40 Years: A Minskyan Assessment." Public Policy Brief No. 78. Annandale-on-Hudson, N.Y.: Levy Economics Institute. June.

Galbraith, J. K. 2000. *Created Unequal: The Crisis in American Pay*. Chicago: University of Chicago Press.

Hawley, J. B. 1981. "Summary of Hyman P. Minsky's Comments on the Carter and Reagan Administrations' Economic Policies and Practices." Notes taken during Minsky's presentation at Southern Illinois University, Carbondale, December 15.

Minsky, H. P. 1965. "The Role of Employment Policy." In Margaret S. Gordon, ed. *Poverty in America*. San Francisco: Chandler Publishing Company. Reprinted as chapter 1 in the present volume.

———. 1968. "Effects of Shifts of Aggregate Demand upon Income Distribution." *American Journal of Agricultural Economics* 50(2): 328–39. Reprinted as chapter 2 in the present volume.

———. 1969. "Policy and Poverty, Part 1"; "Policy and Poverty, Part 2"; "Policy and Poverty, Part 3." Draft manuscript. Papers 8, 9, 10. Hyman P. Minsky Archive, Levy Economics Institute, Annandale-on-Hudson, N.Y. Reprinted as chapter 3 in the present volume.

———. 1972a. "Where the American Economy—and Economists—Went Wrong." Revised text of a talk prepared for delivery at Southern Illinois University, Carbondale, May 20, 1971. Paper 428 ("Third Version"). Hyman P. Minsky Archive, Levy Economics Institute, Annandale-on-Hudson, N.Y. Reprinted as chapter 5 in the present volume.

———. 1972b. "Economic Issues in 1972: A Perspective." Paper presented at a symposium on the economics of the presidential candidates, Department of Economics, Washington University, St. Louis, October 6. Paper 427. Hyman P. Minsky Archive, Levy Economics Institute, Annandale-on-Hudson, N.Y.

———. 1973. "The Strategy of Economic Policy and Income Distribution." *The Annals of the American Academy of Political and Social Science* 409 (September): 92–101.

———. 1975. "The Poverty of Economic Policy." Paper presented at the Graduate Institute of Cooperative Leadership, University of Missouri, Columbia, July 14. Paper 426. Hyman P. Minsky Archive, Levy Economics Institute, Annandale-on-Hudson, N.Y. Reprinted as chapter 6 in the present volume.

———. 1986. *Stabilizing an Unstable Economy*. New Haven: Yale University Press.

Papadimitriou, D. B. 1999. "Full Employment Has Not Been Achieved. Full Employment Policy: Theory and Practice." Public Policy Brief No. 53. Annandale-on-Hudson, N.Y.: Levy Economics Institute. July.

Pigeon, M., and L. R. Wray. 2000. "Can a Rising Tide Raise All Boats? Evidence from the Clinton-Era Expansion." *Journal of Economic Issues* 34(4): 811–45.

Public Papers of the Presidents: Lyndon Baines Johnson, 1963–64. Washington, D.C.: Government Printing Office, 1965, 1: 375–80.

Russell, J. 2004. *Economics, Bureaucracy, and Race: How Keynesians Misguided the War on Poverty*. New York: Columbia University Press.

Tobin, J. 1966. "The Intellectual Revolution in U.S. Policy Making." Noel Buxton Lectures. London: Longmans for the University of Essex.

Wray, L. R. 1997. "Government as Employer of Last Resort: Full Employment without Inflation." Working Paper No. 213. Annandale-on-Hudson, N.Y.: Levy Economics Institute. November.

———. 1998. *Understanding Modern Money: The Key to Full Employment and Price Stability*. Northampton, Mass.: Edward Elgar.

Chapter 1

The Role of Employment Policy* (1965)

Introduction

The war against poverty is a conservative rebuttal to an ancient challenge of the radicals, that capitalism necessarily generates "poverty in the midst of plenty." This war intends to eliminate poverty by changing people, rather than the economy. Thus the emphasis, even in the Job Corps, is upon training or indoctrination to work rather than on the job and the task to be performed. However, this approach, standing by itself, cannot end poverty. All it can do is give the present poor a better chance at the jobs that exist: it can spread poverty more fairly. A necessary ingredient of any war against poverty is a program of job creation; and it has never been shown that a thorough program of job creation, taking people as they are, will not, by itself, eliminate a large part of the poverty that exists.

The war against poverty cannot be taken seriously as long as the Administration and the Congress tolerate a 5 percent unemployment rate and frame monetary and fiscal policy with a target of eventually achieving a 4 percent unemployment rate. Only if there are more jobs than available workers over a broad spectrum of occupations and locations can we hope to make a dent on poverty by way of income from employment. To achieve and sustain tight labor markets in the United States requires bolder, more imaginative, and more consistent use of expansionary monetary and fiscal policy to create jobs than we have witnessed to date.

Incidentally, tight labor markets, by making all labor something of value, will go far to building morale among our urban and rural poor. The community facilities program may be a poor substitute for tight labor markets, even for the social objectives it is trying to achieve.

The war against poverty must not depend solely, or even primarily, upon changing people, but it must be directed toward

---

* Reprinted from Margaret S. Gordon, ed. 1965. *Poverty in America*. Proceedings of a national conference held at the University of California, Berkeley, February 26–28, 1965. San Francisco: Chandler Publishing Company.

changing the system. However, the changes required are not those that the traditional radicals envisage. Rather, they involve a commitment to the maintenance of tight full employment and the adjustment of institutions, so that the gains from full employment are not offset by undue inflation and the perpetuation of obsolete practices.

To anyone who has a deep commitment to a liberal pluralistic democracy, a policy of changing the system rather than changing people is most attractive.

Job creation in the context of the American economy means the sophisticated use of expansionary monetary and fiscal policies. Irrational prejudices, to which even the recent highly professional Councils of Economic Advisers have catered, exist against spending, deficits, and easy money. Ignoring these prejudices, are there any serious barriers against using expansionary aggregate demand–generating policies to achieve tight full employment? In addition, if barriers do exist, can expansionary policies be designed which get around or over them? These are the problems upon which this paper will focus.

Other papers at this conference have considered the various definitions as well as the characteristics of poverty in America. We will just note that the Council of Economic Advisers estimated that in 1963 the heads of 30 percent of the families living in poverty were employed all year and another 30 percent were employed part of the year (CEA 1965, 166, Table 21). A program of ending poverty by generating tight full employment will mainly affect these families, as well as those which will have members drawn into the labor force as a result of jobs being available.

It is also estimated that the heads of some 40 percent of the families living in poverty were not in the labor force during 1963. Obviously, expanded, improved, and modernized programs of transfer payments and income in kind for the aged, the infirm, the disabled, and needy children are necessary. As I see it, this has little to do with the War on Poverty; it has mainly to do with our national conscience and affection for man. Simple decency calls for a system of transfer payments and income in kind for the casebook citizens that lifts their lives well above any "poverty line."

This paper is almost exclusively concerned with the problem of generating enough job opportunities of the right kind, at the right place, and with sufficiently high incomes so that all who are willing and able to work can earn enough from jobs to maintain themselves and those for whom they are responsible at a level above some poverty line. Some adjustments and additions to our system of transfer payments may be required; in particular, family allowances may be in order. However, from the perspective of this paper, such changes are peripheral elements; the fundamental element in any war against poverty is jobs.

Of course, sane adults should be free to choose poverty, but no one should have poverty thrust upon him.

Tight Full Employment

The single most important step toward ending poverty in America would be the achieving and sustaining of tight full employment. Tight full employment exists when over a broad cross-section of occupations, industries, and locations, employers, at going wages and salaries, would prefer to employ more workers than they in fact do. Tight full employment is vital for an antipoverty campaign. It not only will eliminate that poverty which is solely due to unemployment, but, by setting off market processes which tend to raise low wages faster than high wages, it will in time greatly diminish the poverty due to low incomes from jobs. In addition, by drawing additional workers into the labor force, tight full employment will increase the number of families with more than one worker. As a result, families now in or close to poverty will move well away from it. There may be a "critical minimum effort" that is needed to move families to a self-maintaining income growth situation, this effort bringing about a sharp move to a position well above poverty. Having multiple earners in a family is one way of achieving this.

That is, there is no better cure for poverty than family income, especially family income earned on a job.

Ending Poverty: Jobs, Not Welfare

There is a need for us to envisage what a tight-full-employment economy in the United States would look like. Many adjustments might be needed. For example, if we know that we can generate as many jobs as there are workers seeking work, then those programs, many of which are legacies of the Great Depression, designed to control the size of the labor force can be eliminated. In fact, the combination of a commitment to tight full employment and the view that income earned on a job is best indicates that programs to expand the labor force are in order.

Serious research on the attributes of tight full employment should be undertaken, not only because it is a weapon in the War on Poverty, but also because it certainly is one of the attributes of any Great Society. In this section only three attributes of tight full employment will be taken up:

1. The size of tight full employment GNP in 1965
2. The effect of tight full employment on relative wages
3. The effect of the transition to tight full employment on the price level

The "interim" employment goal set four long years ago by the Heller Council of Economic Advisers and reaffirmed by the Ackley Council this year is a 4 percent unemployment rate. On the basis of Swedish and other European experience, this is a very slack employment goal. Even if we allow for considerably greater voluntary mobility and random industrial changes in the United States than prevail in Europe, the Swedish equivalent unemployment rate in the United States might be a measured 2.5 percent unemployment rate (Table 1.1). As an interim definition of tight full employment, I shall use a 2.5 percent unemployment rate. This is lower than the measured annual rate for any year since World War II.

The Council of Economic Advisers, which has been congratulating itself for the performance of the economy in 1964, admits that even with its slack 4 percent definition of full employment, the gap between the potential and actual gross national product was $27 billion in 1964.

Table 1.1 Unemployment Rate, by Month, for Sweden, 1956–63 (in percent)*

Year	Jan.	Feb.	Mar.	Apr.	May	June	July	Aug.	Sept.	Oct.	Nov.	Dec.
1956	2.4	3.6	2.4	2.1	1.3	0.7	0.5	0.7	0.7	0.9	1.3	1.9
1957	2.9	2.6	2.6	2.7	1.9	1.2	0.8	0.9	0.9	1.2	1.7	2.7
1958	3.8	3.6	3.6	3.8	2.6	1.3	1.0	1.3	1.3	1.7	2.4	3.3
1959	4.3	3.4	2.6	2.7	1.9	1.2	1.0	1.2	1.2	1.3	1.6	1.8
1960	2.8	2.5	2.0	1.9	1.2	0.8	0.6	0.8	0.8	0.8	1.1	1.4
1961	2.1	2.0	1.5	1.6	1.1	0.7	0.5	0.7	0.7	0.9	1.2	1.4
1962	2.1	2.2	2.0	1.9	1.3	0.8	0.6	0.8	0.8	1.0	1.2	1.3
1963	3.6	2.5	1.9	1.8	1.1	0.7	0.6	0.8	0.9	—	—	—

* The percentage unemployed is based on the number of registered unemployed within the unemployment insurance system. This number is considerably less than the total number of unemployed. Sample surveys of the labor force are also taken in order to gain more complete information about the number of unemployed. The estimate of the total percentage of all unemployed as opposed to the actual percentage of insured registrants who are unemployed indicates a minor upward revision is necessary in the percentages in the table. For example, the estimated unemployment rate for all workers in November 1961 was 1.7 percent, compared to 1.2 percent for workers covered by unemployment insurance. To adjust Swedish unemployment rates to American definitions, an upward adjustment of about 0.3 to 0.5 percent is necessary.

Sources: Sammanställning Arbetsmarknadstabeller, Kungl. Arbetsmarknadsstyrelsen, Stockholm, October 1963; Schnitzer (1964), 16

What would GNP be in a tight-full-employment United States in 1965? The forecast GNP is $660 billion, but the Council does not expect any reduction in the unemployment rate. Okun's rule of thumb is that for every 1 percentage point decline in the measured unemployment rate there is roughly a 3 percent increase in measured GNP (Okun 1962). If we apply his rule to the difference between 5.2 percent and 2.5 percent unemployment rates, we get a gap of $53 billion. If we modify Okun's rule so that it holds only for unemployment rates down to 4 percent, after which there is a one-one relation between percentage point declines in the unemployment rate and the percentage increase in GNP, we get a gap of $34 billion. No matter how it is estimated, the gap is much larger than the $11 to $12 billion which has been used as the amount it would take to raise the incomes of all those now living in poverty above the poverty line.

The pattern of relative wages in the United States reflects the past of the economy and present institutions as well as present labor market conditions. It is important to recall that relative wages are related to relative value productivities, and there is an interrelation between relative wages and relative prices.

The general rule seems to be that during periods of extreme labor market tightness wage differentials narrow, and that during periods of slack they increase.[1] The widening of the differential during a period of increasing slack in the labor market is illustrated by the relative gross average hourly earnings in the primary metal industry and in retail trade.

Since World War II, the ratio of primary metal to retail trade hourly earnings has risen from 1.54 to 1.70. In 1962, average hourly earnings in retail trade were $1.75, which is close to the $1.50 per hour that marks the poverty line. In 1947, wages in retail trade were two-thirds of those in the primary metal trade. If the same ratio ruled in 1962, given primary metal industry wages of almost $3.00 per hour, wages in retail trade would have been about $2.00 per hour. This is substantially farther above the poverty line than the $1.75 per hour that in fact prevailed. That is, if the 1947 wage ratio had been maintained, the contribution of retail trade employment to poverty would have been much smaller.

The Role of Employment Policy (1965)

The cohesiveness of relative wages and the importance of key trade union contracts in setting a pattern for wage increases depend upon the overall tightness in the labor market. In particular, wage gains in industries with weak trade unions—such as textiles—or with essentially no trade unions—such as retail trade—will keep up with or even improve on the bargains struck in highly organized industries such as steel and automobiles only if the labor market is tight.[2]

Between 1947 and 1962, employment in the primary metal industry fell by some 180,000, while employment in retail trade rose by more than 1.3 million. Over this period, as we have seen, the ratio of primary metal wages to retail trade wages rose from 1.54 to 1.70; that is, wages in primary metals rose relative to wages in retail trade, even though employment in primary metals was decreasing while employment in retail trade was increasing. This indicates that it was supply conditions rather than demand conditions that affected relative wages; for if it were demand conditions, the rising "demand" for labor in retail trade as compared with the primary metal industry would have led to retail wages increasing relative to primary metal industry.

Conceptually, we can think of two sets of industries—high- and low-wage industries. High-wage industries exist because the employers want to be able to "select" their workers. Perhaps they invest so much in training or are so vulnerable to worker dissatisfaction that they are willing to pay premium wages in order to be able to select their workers and keep them happy. Since they award a prize whenever they hire, these high-wage industries have an infinitely elastic labor supply at their going wage (L_s in the diagram on p. 8).

A simple model which generates the observed type of relative wage behavior follows (Figure 1.1).

The supply curve of labor to the low-wage industries is upward sloping—but its position depends upon the number of workers employed by the high-wage industries. Thus, if employment by the high-wage industries increases, the supply curve of workers to the low-wage industries shifts to the left; and if the high-wage employment decreases, the low-wage industry's labor supply curve shifts to the right. If the demand curve for high-wage industry shifts to

Figure 1.1

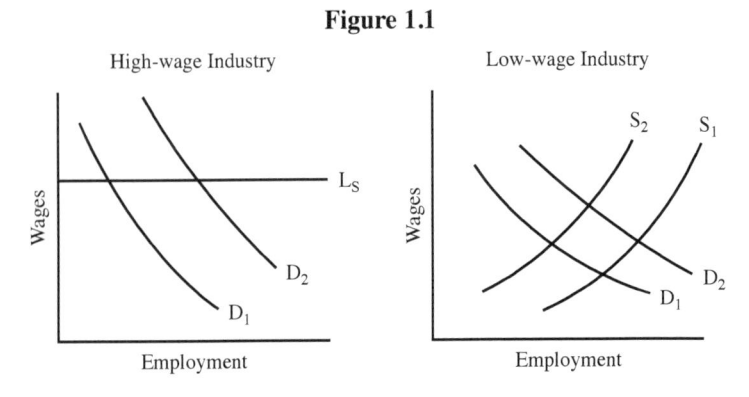

High-wage Industry — Wages vs Employment, with curves L_S, D_1, D_2.

Low-wage Industry — Wages vs Employment, with curves S_1, S_2, D_1, D_2.

D_1 from D_2, the supply curve of labor to the low-wage industry shifts from S_2 to S_1. As a result, wages fall and employment increases in the low-wage industry.

If, on the other hand, aggregate demand is increased, so that the demand for labor in both the high- and low-wage industries rises from D_1 to D_2, then the supply curve in the low-wage industry also shifts, this time to the left of S_2. Total employment in the low-wage industry may rise or fall, depending upon the reaction of labor force participation rates to higher wages and improved job availability, but its wages will rise, while wages in the high-wage industry would remain constant.

This "model" of the labor market is static. It ignores the fact that in general real wages will rise over time. We can, as a first approximation, assume that in the high-wage industry money wages will rise at the same rate as labor productivity. Thus, in a dynamic context, the fall in low wages, associated with labor market slack, and the rise in low wages, associated with labor market tightness, must be interpreted as a rise or fall relative to wages in the high-wage industry.

One of the intermediate policy objectives of the antipoverty campaign should be to facilitate the rise of wages in low-wage industries while constraining the rise of wages in high-wage industries. A problem that arises in implementing such an incomes policy is that it is also necessary to constrain the rate of increase of

The Role of Employment Policy (1965)

nonwage incomes. The proud boast of Gardner Ackley, chairman of the Council of Economic Advisers, that corporate profits after taxes rose by 18 percent in 1964, shows either that some policymakers are not serious about eliminating poverty, or a strange belief on their part that poverty has nothing to do with income distribution.

The antipoverty campaign carries an implicit commitment to a rapid increase of those wages that are close to or below the poverty line. A more rapid increase in these wages than in the physical productivity of the workers implies a rise in the prices of the products or services that use these workers. For the measured price level to remain constant, offsetting decreases in some other prices—the prices for the products of high-wage industries—would have to take place. That is, for price-level stability, wages in high-wage industries would have to rise by less than the increases in the productivity of their workers, and management in these often oligopolistic industries would have to pass this decline in unit costs on to their customers.

The existence of nonlabor costs and incomes makes the programming of declining prices when wages rise less than labor productivity difficult. Assume that the productivity of labor increases in our high-wage industries, but wages are kept constant. Let us also assume that this is a truly disembodied increase in productivity: no increase in the capital stock or visible change in technique occurred. If prices per unit fell by the same percentage as did wages per unit, then gross profits per unit of output would also fall by the same ratio. However, the capital value of the firm and its ability to meet contractual financial commitments depends not upon the mark-up on wages, but rather on the flow of gross profits after taxes. Only if the elasticity of demand for the product is equal to or greater than one will such a fall in relative prices lead to a gross profit flow that is large enough to maintain capital values and meet financial commitments.

As firms tend to be risk averters, the usual assumption they will make is that the demand for their output is inelastic. They will attempt to cut prices by a smaller percentage than the fall in their labor costs, thereby raising profit margins. Given the deviations from competitive conditions that exist in much of our economy, they will succeed in this effort. Thus, the distribution of income between profits and wages will shift to profits. This is not desirable both on policy and aggregate demand grounds, and given the generally strong position of trade unions in high-wage industries, it is also not stable.

The outcome we can hope for with tight full employment and a commitment for low wages to rise more rapidly than high wages, is for high wages to follow some productivity guideline. As a result, prices of the products of the high-wage industries will not fall, and prices of the products of the low-wage industries will rise. The transfer of a larger proportion of the overall productivity gains to the workers in the low-wage industries will take place by way of rising relative prices for the output of the low-wage industries.

We can look at the effect of relative wage changes in another way. The high-wage worker and other affluent citizens have been subsidized, by way of low product prices, by the poor. If the poverty campaign results in tight full employment, it will lead to a cost-push inflation; for the removal of the subsidy will lead to a rise in the measured price level.

This inflation is a phenomenon of the transition from a slack- to a tight-full-employment economy. Once a tight-full-employment economy is generated and sustained, this source of inflationary pressure will cease. (Whether or not there is inflationary pressure in a sustained tight labor market will be discussed in the next section.) Given the highly emotional and thus irrational opposition to inflation that exists, those committed to the elimination of poverty in America will have to prepare to hold to their objectives while this transitional inflation occurs.

Incidentally, the position that the Administration (as well as many economists) has been taking—that the likelihood that inflation will occur increases as the unemployment rate gets to or below 4 percent[3]—is in the nature of a self-fulfilling prophesy. By repeatedly stating this view, they are "brainwashing" business and labor into believing that inflation is unavoidable at low unemployment rates. If business and labor begin to act as if inflation will take place once unemployment rates are down, then inflation will take place.

The Role of Employment Policy (1965)

Part of the task of those committed to the success of the War on Poverty is to enlighten all concerned that the rectification of relative wages—which is necessary for the success of the war—will be accompanied by a rise in the measured price level. This inflation is quite a different kettle of fish from an inflation which either maintains or perversely changes relative wages.

Our slogan must be: not all inflations are bad!

Barriers to Using Aggregate Demand as an Antipoverty Measure

There is no doubt that the expected aggregate demand for 1965 is insufficient to generate tight full employment. A tight-full-employment GNP would be in the neighborhood of $700 billion. The Council of Economic Advisers forecast a GNP and thus an aggregate demand of $660 billion for 1965. They also predicted that no appreciable reduction in unemployment rates would be achieved. The estimated $660 billion GNP is below the slack-employment definition of capacity the Council uses. A minimal aggregate demand policy for 1965 consistent with the objectives of the war against poverty is to use monetary and fiscal policy to raise demand to at least the 4 percent unemployment capacity level, if not the tight-full-employment capacity level.

Three purported barriers to the effectiveness of measures to increase aggregate demand in the War on Poverty will be discussed. One is that labor and product markets will operate so that an increase in aggregate demand will be dissipated in price increases. The second barrier is that urban white non-aged poor families are in the "tail" of the income distribution, so that an upward shift of median income will not appreciably reduce the proportion living in poverty. The third is that a rise in income, with or without an accompanying rise in prices, will quickly bring on a balance of payments crisis.

These three barriers are quite different. The first two are based upon technical characteristics of the economy; the third, the balance of payments barrier, is based upon legislated institutions and a policy objective. The dissipation via inflation argument depends upon assumptions as to the nature of labor demand and labor supply. The income distribution argument follows from an assumption that a move to tight full employment is equivalent to growth at full employment insofar as the distribution of income is concerned. These two arguments lead to the propositions that further increases in demand will merely result in inflation and in improving the lot of the already well-to-do.

As will be indicated below, it is not certain that these two barriers exist. Thus, they do not constitute a good reason for failing to take additional measures to increase aggregate demand, such as measures to ease the money market or an additional tax cut. Such programs should be adopted even though it can be shown that they would not be as effective in eliminating poverty as a correctly distributed increase in spending. However, they can be put into operation more quickly and thus should be used. If these technical barriers do exist, then the only cost of the experiment would be a once-and-for-all increase in the price level.

However, there is a real barrier to such an experiment with aggregate demand. It is the impact not only on our balance of payments, but also on our position as an international banker. Monetary ease as a means of expanding our economy is ruled out by the need to keep foreign (and domestic) short-term deposits in the United States. Since convertibility of European currencies has been achieved, the location of certain deposits is sensitive to covered interest rate differentials. Thus, the active use of monetary policy to expand demand is constrained by the banking aspect of our balance of payments problem. Under present arrangements, the monetary authorities must see to it that United States short-term interest rates are high enough to keep short-term balances—foreign as well as domestic—in the United States.

Thus the only really available devices for expanding aggregate demand are fiscal.

Underlying the Council of Economic Advisers' commitment to a 4 percent "interim" unemployment goal is a belief that the "Phillips curve" for the United States is such that rapidly rising wages and prices occur whenever United States measured unemployment is below 4 percent.[4] That demand increases are dissipated by price increases when unemployment is below 4 percent is not a well-substantiated argument. In the first place, the only type of tight labor market that has ever been observed in the United States is the transitional type. We move to tightness and back away. We have never observed the results of moving to a tight labor market and staying there. The evidence from World War II is not relevant; for unconstrained demand was far greater than potential supply, and, of course, great premiums were being paid to achieve desired labor mobility.

The evidence from Europe should be examined from the point of view of what labor market institutions would be needed in order to constrain inflationary pressures under conditions of tight full employment where the condition is expected to persist. It seems as if even in Sweden there still is a wage rate–unemployment relation similar to the Phillips curve, although, of course, the Swedish government does not use this type of inflation as an excuse for not maintaining tight labor markets.

The argument that tight full employment cannot be achieved by measures to increase demand is a structuralist argument. For the standard income determination models, it is assumed that labor is homogeneous and fluid. In such models, as long as there is any unemployment, the labor supply to any and all occupations is infinitely elastic at the same going wage rate. It does not matter how demand is increased: no matter where or what kind of initial impact occurs and no matter what the pattern of final output may be, the employment and wage effects are the same.

Obviously, labor is not homogeneous and fluid. The gestation period of a worker with particular skills in a particular place may be quite time consuming and the gestation process quite costly. At every date there is a need not only to generate the right kinds of labor, but also to make do with the available labor force. In theory, slight changes in relative supply prices of the various kinds, or qualities, of labor could lead to a considerable amount of substitution in production; that is, in making do. Such substitution in production would tend to narrow wage differentials. However, for many outputs the technical possibilities of substitution are limited.

Since labor is actually heterogeneous and viscous, the efficacy of different demand-generating instruments in raising employment depends upon where the initial change in final demand takes place, what the immediate derived demands are, and what the ultimate change in final demand is. In addition, it does not pay to train workers unless it is felt that the demand for a particular type of trained labor will be sustained. Thus, the expected length of time for which labor markets will be tight is a determinant of the extent to which labor will be trained to conform to the pattern of demand.

The standard theory of aggregate demand generation glosses over the differences in effect of the various demand-generating policy actions. Monetary ease, increased spending, and decreased taxes are perfect substitutes insofar as their effects upon GNP, employment, and prices are concerned. A conventional argument is that fiscal ease can be used to offset the effects of tight money; and seemingly, tax reductions are perfect substitutes for spending programs. But this, in fact, is not so.

All of the policy instruments have "what kind" as well as "how much" dimensions. Proper attention to the "what kind" is necessary in using monetary-fiscal measures, and the "what kind" should be determined in the light of the contribution it makes to the war against poverty.

As was mentioned earlier, the use of expansionary monetary policy is constrained by the international position of the dollar. Thus, we need not discuss it, except to note that the path from monetary ease to aggregate demand is not particularly favorable for the War on Poverty.

The Administration emphasized tax reductions in its expansionary fiscal policy of 1964 and again in 1965. From the perspective of the war against poverty, this is a poor choice. The initial impact of tax reductions is through the increased spending power of those with incomes. The present poor are not direct beneficiaries; they benefit only to the extent that jobs are created, by way of the spending of the affluent, that they can get. Given the regional and ethnic concentration of poverty and income, the immediate demand for labor resulting from the spending by the beneficiaries of the tax cut will have only a small component of demand for the services of the present poor. From the point of view of the poverty campaign, it matters where the initial spending takes place. The "trickle down upon them" approach of tax cuts is not efficient; Harlem is not Scarsdale.

In order to use expansionary monetary and fiscal policy in an efficient program against poverty, it is necessary to recognize the heterogeneity and the viscosity of the labor force. This means that the emphasis should be upon the spending side of fiscal policy, and an object of the spending should be to have the largest primary and secondary impact upon the present poor. Thus, spending should be directed at the communities with low incomes, and the spending programs should directly employ the low-income worker.

If we look at the pattern of increases in government spending in the postwar period, it has been biased against the poor. The most rapidly growing sector of federal government spending has been upon research and development, which has been growing at the rate of 20 percent per year. This has biased labor demand toward the highly educated and well trained. Another rapidly growing sector of final demand has been in education. The number of teachers increased by 48 percent in the decade of the 1950s, while the labor force grew by 14 percent. These policy-determined changes in the composition of final demand help to explain why the belief has grown that from now on job markets necessarily will be biased to the highly trained. A different emphasis in final government demand would have changed the trends in employment. After all, during the Great Depression the lament was, "I used to be on the daisy chain, but now I am a chain store daisy."

That is, there is nothing sacred about the pattern of demand for labor.

As a result of economic growth, the median family income of nonfarm white families whose head was aged less than 65 years had increased to $6,582 by 1960, and less than 10 percent of this group had incomes in the poverty range. Even though the incidence of poverty in this class is small, it is a large group and contains some 30 percent of all the poor. Locke Anderson advances the argument that for this large group of the poor, further increases in overall income, resulting from economic growth, will not appreciably decrease the incidence of poverty (Anderson 1964). He based his argument on the fact that, in terms of the distribution of income, these present poor are in the long attenuated tail of the income distribution. An upward shift of the entire distribution will not draw a large number of these poor across the poverty line.

However, there is a difference between the growth of income that occurs in a persistently slack labor market, such as we have had in the recent past, and the shift from a slack- to a tight-full-employment economy. There is no necessity for a tight-full-employment economy to grow any faster than a slack economy. The emphasis upon growth of the Heller era (which is persisting now that Gardner Ackley is chairman of the Council of Economic Advisers) was a mistake. What needs to be emphasized is that the shift from a slack- to a tight-full-employment economy would be accompanied by a once-and-for-all jump in GNP and a change in relative wages favoring the low-wage industries. That is, the increase in average income which would occur during this period would be of such a nature as to reduce substantially the lower tail of the income distribution. Thus, the shift to tight full employment would lead to a marked reduction in poverty. This would be followed by a further slow decrease in poverty under conditions of continued growth with the new income distribution.

This can be illustrated by referring again to the argument about the relative wages of primary metal workers and retail trade workers. In 1962, the average hourly wage of primary metal workers was approximately $3.00, and retail trade workers averaged $1.75 per hour; that is, the median annual income was roughly $6,000 in primary metals, and approximately $3,500 in retail trade. Given this median income, a very small percentage of the primary metal industry workers would be likely to earn less than $3,000 per year, whereas a substantially greater percentage of the workers in retail trade would fall below the same poverty line. The change in relative wages which would occur in a tight labor market would increase the average annual income of retail trade workers relative to that of primary metal workers and markedly reduce the percentage of retail trade workers with incomes below the poverty line. On the other hand, an increase of, let us say, $500 in annual incomes of primary metal workers would not markedly change the number lying below the poverty line.

In addition, if the high aggregate demand resulted in shifting workers from low- to high-wage industries, then the incidence of poverty would be markedly reduced; i.e., the relative weights of the different occupations and industries in the determination of the overall income distribution would change as tight full employment became the way of life.

Thus there is no real conflict between the proposition that tight full employment will lower poverty markedly and the proposition that further growth of capacity GNP will not quickly reduce poverty.

Fundamentally, tight full employment is inconsistent with the Administration's balance of payments objectives. An international monetary system with fixed exchange rates based upon the dollar is incompatible with tight full employment and the rapid elimination of poverty in the United States. If, for example, the marginal propensity to import equals the average propensity when imports are 4 percent of GNP, then a GNP $50 billion larger than that achieved in 1964 would have resulted in additional imports of about $2 billion. Moreover, the move to tight labor markets would entail a rise in prices, which would further affect the balance of payments. A balance of payments deficit of $5 billion in any one year tends to generate a flight from the dollar, and a tight-full-employment economy would tend to create such a deficit.

To a considerable extent, ever since 1958 the needs of the dollar standard have acted as a constraint upon domestic income. We have not had tight labor markets because of the peculiar bind that the dollar is in internationally. It is apparently appropriate to allude to William Jennings Bryan by saying that, in part, the cross that the American poor bear is made of gold.

A Program against Poverty

The reason we need to understand the barriers to pursuing a tight-full-employment policy is to enable us to design efficient policy strategies to overcome these barriers—not to enable us to shrug our shoulders and prepare excuses for failure. In this section some suggestions will be made as to how the federal government's tax, spending, and monetary controls can be used to generate tight full employment, although, obviously, it will not be possible to include a complete catalogue of what should be considered.

The solution to the gold standard barrier is simple: get rid of the gold standard. If, for some subtle reasons understood only by bankers, the Department of State, and the Treasury, we cannot do this, then we can buy economic breathing room by raising the price of gold. An even better move would be to announce once and for all that a "dollar is a dollar," that the US Treasury will sell gold as long as it has any, but it will no longer buy gold. Within a very short time an international monetary system rooted firmly in the dollar's ability to command goods and services in the US would arise—and we would be able to proceed to build the Great Society at home.

To the extent that we continue to try to live with the gold standard, expansionary monetary policy is not available as a weapon to achieve tight full employment. In fact, monetary constraint might have to be increased as income increases to compensate, as far as the balance of payments is concerned, for the greater volume of imports which accompanies the higher GNP.[5]

On the other hand, the argument that more rapid expansion will not improve the relative position of the poor is *not* a real barrier to more vigorous monetary and fiscal measures; it just asserts that it will not be effective. The answer to this objection is "Let us try tight full employment and see what happens."

The function of intervention in a free enterprise economy is to make the economy behave so as to achieve the best of attainable situations. "Best" often implies a choice, or at least a trade-off, among objectives. The war against poverty as a "new" policy objective implies that the relative weights given to other policy objectives need to be reconsidered. In particular, the war against poverty requires both a definition of full employment as tight full employment and the inclusion of a relative wage or relative income policy objective in the set of policy goals.

Economic theory asserts that no appreciable inflation will occur until aggregate labor demand exceeds aggregate labor supply—the homogeneity and fluidity of labor will guarantee this result. However, labor is not homogeneous and fluid, and, in addition, effective production functions seem to be such that marked substitution among types of labor does not take place in response to small wage differentials. Thus, economic policy should devise interventions that make labor more homogeneous and that generate demand for the unemployed, relatively low-wage workers.

The emphasis upon job training, labor relocation, and other similar programs is intended to make labor more homogeneous. However, there are limits to the capacity of such programs to transform particular types of labor which are in excess supply into the types that are in excess demand. Thus, as excess demand appears for particular classes of labor, further expansion of demand for labor should be concentrated on other types of labor. Once generalized excess supply of labor disappears, the choice between tax cuts and government spending as alternative fiscal stimuli becomes important. Whereas the ability to stimulate the demand for particular types of labor by way of generalized tax cuts is limited, the ability to tailor-make government spending to conform to the particular excess supplies is not limited. In other words, although tax cuts and spending are largely equivalent in stimulating recovery from a depression, they are not fully equivalent in generating full employment during a period when a substantial amount of unemployment is the result of structural changes.

Along with job training and labor relocation policies, programs to encourage the substitution of labor that is now in excess supply for labor now in excess demand should also be undertaken. Aside from industry relocation, such programs might very well take the form of breaking complex jobs down into simpler jobs—for example, using park patrolmen as supplements to completely trained police. If we ever do get an urban extension service (comparable to the agricultural extension service), one of its tasks might be to look at an area's demand and supply of labor to determine how complex jobs might be divided into jobs within the grasp of the existing unemployed.

Dynamic economics is primarily concerned with differential reaction and gestation periods. We are learning that what happens to a child between the ages of three to five is of vital importance in determining the capabilities of the adult. Thus, preschool training is necessary to break the vicious circle of poverty. But if this view is true, then it takes 18 to 20 years to realize the benefits from such programs. Similarly, we cannot stimulate the demand for labor of a 20-year-old high school dropout by increasing appropriations for the National Institutes of Health, the Atomic Energy Commission, space programs, and the like. Programs must be designed which hold out a promise of a useful and productive life for our high school dropouts.

Spending programs aimed at directly employing those in the labor market who are poor, and opening up job opportunities for second earners in the families of the present poor, would have a strong impact upon poverty. Only in the second and subsequent rounds of spending following the original round will there be a demand for other kinds of labor, and, as indicated earlier, primary jobs for residents of Harlem will generate retail and service jobs in Harlem. The present poor are more likely to get such jobs than they are to get similar jobs in the suburbs.

The New Deal, with its WPA, NYA, and CCC*, took workers as they were, and generated jobs for them. Sweden today generates public works jobs for the seasonally unemployed in its north country. We could easily do the same in areas such as northern Wisconsin and Michigan, and for poor farm families throughout the country. The resurrection of WPA and allied projects should be a major weapon of the War on Poverty.

Note that the WPA was a labor-intensive approach to unemployment, and it did tailor-make its projects to the capabilities of the available labor. There was another expansionary spending approach during the depression—PWA were its "initials" during at least part of its life—which went in for massive public works. Public works are favored by the trade union movement and by contractors as

---

* Works Progress Administration, National Youth Administration, and Civilian Conservation Corps, respectively.

The Role of Employment Policy (1965)

a solution to unemployment programs. In the context of the war against poverty, programs of expanding standard public works are inefficient; for they mean providing jobs for already affluent workers. "Public works" is not much better than a tax cut as an anti-poverty measure.

Work should be made available to all who want work at the national minimum wage. This would be a wage support law, analogous to the price supports for agricultural products. It would replace the minimum wage law; for, if work is available to all at the minimum wage, no labor will be available to private employers at a wage lower than this minimum. That is, the problem of coverage of occupations would disappear. To qualify for employment at these terms, all that would be necessary would be to register at the local public employment office.

Various national government agencies, as well as local and state government agencies, would be eligible to obtain this labor. They would bid for labor by submitting their projects, and a local "evaluation" board would determine priorities among projects. Because skilled, technical, and supervisory personnel are needed, the projects should be allowed to average something like $4,000 per worker. The federal government should put in some funds for materials, but the allocation for materials should be a fraction of the labor costs — let us say, 25 percent.

Not so long ago, economists and other social scientists thought disarmament was a possibility. Daniel B. Suits used the Michigan model of the United States economy to estimate employment effects of various alternative programs. He found that if the government used $1 billion to employ some 260,000 workers — i.e., a spending program concentrating on low-income jobs — the result would be a rise of 322,000 in employment (Table 1.2).

Let us assume that there are some two million more unemployed than there would be if we enjoyed tight full employment. Assume that the remaining "2.5 percent" unemployed are short-term transitional unemployed who would not take advantage of such a program; standard unemployment insurance is sufficient protection for these unemployed. An expenditure of $7 billion per year, resulting

Table 1.2 Multipliers for Selected Activities (in billions of dollars)

	Government Purchases	Government Employment*	Federal Income Tax Level	Federal Income Tax Yield	Social Security Transactions	Private Investment in Plant and Equipment
	+1.0	+1.0	+1.0	+1.0	+1.0	+1.0
Gross National Product	1.304	1.903	−1.119	−1.798	0.825	1.690
Consumption Expenditure	0.295	0.738	−0.915	−1.470	0.674	0.382
Unemployment Insurance Benefits	−0.160	−0.390	0.091	0.146	−0.069	−0.137
Tax Receipts						
Federal	0.458	0.220	0.622	1.000	0.274	0.586
State and Local	0.030	0.034	−0.045	−0.072	0.033	0.058
Social Insurance	0.030	0.051	−0.024	−0.039	0.018	0.038
Employment (millions of persons)	0.089	0.322	−0.076	−0.122	0.056	0.115

* Additional government wage expenditure of $1.0 billion to hire 260,000 employees.

Source: Suits (1963), 104

in direct employment of 1,820,000, on the basis of Suits's estimates, would eliminate the excess unemployment. However, with a wage support law, workers making below the minimum wage—including many low-income farmers and people not now in the labor force—would join the program. Perhaps a $10 billion gross expenditure employing some 2,600,000 workers would be a more appropriate initial amount for the program.

Given that some 25 percent of the labor cost would be available for material spending, the gross cost would be $12.5 billion per year. This would lead to a rise of $22.3 billion in GNP. Although it is a relatively unimportant consideration, federal tax receipts would rise by $3.3 billion; thus, the net cost of such a program would be some $9.2 billion per year.

This path to tight full employment generates a GNP that is smaller than the estimated tight-full-employment GNP used earlier. This is so because these workers are fed into the value of output at less than the median labor income.

Needed improvements of transfer and income in kind programs might cost an additional $5 billion per year. Thus, the total cost of a meaningful war against poverty might be $17.5 billion per year.

Incidentally, many of the proposed community development type projects might fit into the set of approved WPA-type projects. Certainly a directive to the local evaluation body to weight such programs highly would be in order.

Once such an artificially created tight labor market existed, the pattern of excess demands for labor resulting from generalized measures to expand aggregate demand would indicate the job training and work relocations that should be undertaken. These training and relocation programs are really valuable within a context of tight labor markets. Lifelong learning for all is a necessary policy objective in our complex and ever-changing economy and society. Programs making this possible and appealing to all should be instituted. But this is not solely or even primarily a concern of the war against poverty.

In the process of achieving tight full employment, low wages in the private sector would be pushed up, hopefully, more quickly than high wages. (If this did not take place, tight full employment would have to be supplemented by an incomes policy.) Under these conditions, the national minimum wage could be raised. If, for example, $3.00 per hour is the median gross wage, the wage support level could be raised over time from its present level of 40 percent of the median wage to 60 percent. However, raising the minimum wage now is not particularly desirable; it is more important, first, to make the present minimum wage effective for all.

Many workers in both private and public employment are paid at or below the poverty line. Since an effective antipoverty war would raise low wages relative to high wages, a question as to whether the rise in wages should be passed on to prices is in order.

For example, such workers as hospital attendants and orderlies require relatively little skill and can be trained easily. They also tend to receive incomes close to the poverty line. To raise their incomes and not raise the price of hospital care, the "public" nature of such employment should be recognized. It would strike a visitor from Mars as odd that in the United States the federal government can support the building and equipping of hospitals, but it cannot support the pay of the operating personnel. A scheme under which the federal government paid a percentage of the wages of workers in industries such as hospitals should be part of our permanent package of price- and income-determining measures.

Another aspect of the problem which I will just mention is that people can become impoverished, even though they are not poor. A skilled worker or an engineer, for example, may lose a job because of technical or program changes. If no fully equivalent job is available, this worker will suffer a capital loss—equivalent to the loss by fire of an uninsured house. Some integration of programs to cope with this dynamic and high-level impoverishment into our unemployment compensation system seems to be in order. Perhaps the capital value of such contract revisions should be available as compensation to victims of technical change.

The line between what is private and what is public is narrow and arbitrary. Subsidized employment opportunities for the present poor and ill-trained are just as useful as subsidized employment opportunities for the people like us in conferences such as this, or in government-supported research institutes. We are rich enough to afford boondoggles for the poor as well as the affluent, and I would expect the gains in welfare to be at least as great, per dollar of expenditure.

To conclude, the way to end the biggest chunk of poverty is to generate jobs at adequate incomes for the people in poverty. Some improvements in transfer payments, such as children's allowances and medical care for all, without means tests, would help; but the basic approach must be to provide jobs for all who are willing and able to work—taking their abilities as they are.

Once tight full employment is achieved, the second step is to generate programs to upgrade workers. I am afraid that in the poverty campaign we have taken the second step without the first, and perhaps this is analogous to the great error-producing sin of infielders—throwing the ball before you have it.

Notes

1. A study which summarizes the evidence with regard to the effect of slack and tightness is Ulman (1965). The illustrative example used here is consistent with the results of Ulman's thorough analysis.
2. Levinson (1960) supports this view.
3. Kermit Gordon, director of the Bureau of the Budget, was cited by the *Wall Street Journal* of February 24, 1965, as holding this view.
4. The "Phillips curve" is a relation between unemployment and wage or price increases. See Phillips (1958). See also Lipsey (1960; 1965) and Samuelson and Solow (1960).
5. Obviously, all of the complexities of the international monetary problem cannot be considered in this paper, where it is but one of many issues. Many suggestions for modifying the present monetary system are being discussed, most of which are designed to bring greater flexibility into the world's monetary arrangements. It is important to note that we have brought "flexibility" into our international monetary arrangements by devices such as the interest rate equalization tax. The question is not one of fixity versus flexibility; rather, it is "what type of flexibility."

Sources

Anderson, W. H. L. 1964. "Trickling Down: The Relationship between Economic Growth and the Extent of Poverty among American Families." *Quarterly Journal of Economics* 78(4): 511–24.

CEA (Council of Economic Advisers). 1965. *Economic Report of the President*. Washington, D.C.: Government Printing Office. January.

Levinson, H. M. 1960. "Postwar Inflation." Study Paper No. 21. In *Employment, Growth, and Price Levels*. Report of the Joint Economic Committee, pursuant to Senate Concurrent Resolution 13, 86th Cong., 1st sess. S. Rep. No. 1043 (January).

Lipsey, R. G. 1960. "The Relation between Unemployment and the Rate of Change of Money Wage Rates in the United Kingdom, 1862–1957: A Further Analysis." *Economica* 27(105): 1–31.

———. 1965. "Structural and Deficient-Demand Unemployment Reconsidered." In A. M. Ross, ed. *Employment Policy and the Labor Market*, 210–55. Berkeley and Los Angeles: University of California Press.

Okun, A. 1962. "Potential G.N.P.: Its Measurement and Significance." In *1962 Proceedings of the Business and Economic Statistics Section*, 98–104. Alexandria, Va.: American Statistical Association.

Phillips, A. W. 1958. "The Relation between Unemployment and the Rate of Change of Money Wage Rates in the United Kingdom, 1861–1957." *Economica* 25(100): 283–99.

Samuelson, P., and R. Solow. 1960. "Analytical Aspects of Anti-Inflation Policy." *American Economic Review* 50(2): 177–94.

Schnitzer, M. 1964. "Economic Policies and Practices." Paper No. 5. In *Unemployment Programs in Sweden*. Report of the Joint Economic Committee. 88th Cong., 2nd sess.

Suits, D. B. 1963. "Econometric Analysis of Disarmament Impacts." In E. Benoit and K. Boulding, eds. *Disarmament and the American Economy*. New York: Harper and Row.

Ulman, L. 1965. "Labor Mobility and the Industrial Wage Structure in the Postwar United States." *Quarterly Journal of Economics* 79(1): 73–97.

Chapter 2

Effects of Shifts of Aggregate Demand upon Income Distribution* (1968)

In the United States a large portion of those living in poverty and an even larger portion of those living close to poverty do so because of the meager income they receive from work. The questions that need answering if, someday, a serious war on poverty is to be mounted relate to the distribution of income and the available policy tools which can affect the distribution of income in the relatively short run. The emphasis upon the short run makes programs based upon accelerated investment in humans irrelevant. It also means that the impact of economic growth upon the extent of poverty (Anderson 1964) is not germane. The policy problem is to affect the distribution of income, given the capacity to produce and the skills and locations embodied in the labor force.

Early in the preparations for a possible war on poverty, I was drawn into discussions dealing with the prospective campaign. My view was summarized in the subtitle of a talk at the Berkeley conference (chapter 1), a subtitle that was too flip for the editor of the published version. The subtitle was "Is This Trip Necessary?" I consciously ignored the poverty of those not expected to be in the labor force, which can be handled only by a sufficiently generous scheme of transfer payments. The argument of the paper, and of some subsequent writings, was that the achievement and sustaining of tight full employment could do almost all of the job of eliminating poverty.

My thesis was that tight full employment would help eliminate poverty in at least two ways: (1) by employing the unemployed and moving part-time workers to the fully employed class, and (2) by fostering labor market conditions such that low wages will increase at a faster rate than high wages.

---

* Presented at the Winter Meeting of the American Farm Economic Association with Allied Social Science Associations, Washington, D.C., December 28–30, 1967. Reprinted with permission from the *American Journal of Agricultural Economics* 50(2): 328–39. Oxford University Press, May 1968.

Tight full employment as I defined it was neither achieved nor sustained during the 1960s. As an interim measure of tight full employment, I suggested a measured unemployment rate of 3.0 percent, considerably below the best we have achieved since 1953 but well above measured rates in Europe. In spite of a war added onto an investment boom, the lowest monthly unemployment rate achieved during the current expansion was 3.5 percent, and we never got far below 3.7 percent for a sustained period.

The events of the expansion indicate that we cannot rely upon "undirected" aggregate demand increases to do the job which I claimed it could do. This is because of two facets of what happened:

1. The crunch of August–September 1966 showed that a sustained expansion, or even sustained growth, breeds "stresses and strains" within the economy which make the continuation of the expansion or growth unlikely. Thus, sustaining tight full employment may require more than just an expansionary monetary and fiscal policy.
2. The distribution of relative wages did not appreciably improve during the expansion of the 1960s.

Thus, it may be that greater attention to the structure of aggregate demand is necessary if a desired change in relative wages is to be achieved. The question is whether "directed" demand can achieve the goal of greater equality or whether a system of direct controls is needed, with or without directed demand.

Income Distribution as a Policy Goal

After the summer of 1967, the "question" of the distribution of income, in all its dimensions and not only as measured money income, should be the leading domestic issue. One way of stating the problem is that there is some maximum inequality to the distribution of a generalized income that is compatible with social stability. It seems clear that a good wording of the leading social imperative is "to assure domestic peace and tranquility."

Effects of Shifts of Aggregate Demand upon Income Distribution (1968)

The maximum inequality consistent with any set of social goals is not invariant. It is useful to conjecture, following Scitovsky[*] (1964), that in a technically sophisticated, highly urbanized society inequality of measured income more truly reflects inequality of real or "subjective" income than in a less sophisticated, rural environment. In the dimensions not measured by the earning and spending of private income, life may be easier and the contributions of public and free goods more evenly distributed in a rural and small-town setting than in our modern cities. Whereas the "inequality" in the distribution of private income may be partially offset by the distribution of free and public goods in some settings, in our modern urban ghettos the coverage of free goods has decreased and public goods typically are distributed so as to aggravate the measured inequality of income. In addition, there are problems of perception and tradition: rural poverty may be associated with a belief in the inevitability of status differences, whereas urban societies are associated with a belief in social and economic mobility.

Another reason why a consensus that equity exists is required is that, in a modern urban society, for a broad set of occupations, public benefits exceed private benefits. The dependence of any particular unit's output upon the smooth working of other units is so obvious that observed difference in income received must correspond to some notion of "fairness."

Roughly speaking, there are two classes of policy instruments which can be used to affect income distribution: one set affects factor payments from production; the other affects disposable income by a system of transfer payments.

There has been much discussion of broadening the tax system to provide transfer payments by right, the so-called negative income tax (Green 1967). Objections to the negative income tax are possible on two planes. One is that if the income guarantee is "adequate," a sizable disincentive effect may exist, therefore decreasing attainable real gross national product. The second set of objections is political and social: the creation of a large class of

---

[*] Tibor Scitovsky.

social remittance men and women is not conducive to either social cohesion or domestic tranquility.

The virtues of the negative income tax are that it eliminates the stigma and costs of caseload welfare, and that in principle it could provide adequate incomes for the economically inactive portion of the population. More nearly adequate welfare and pension schemes and, in addition, some way of guaranteeing such income protection as a right are necessary. But it is an admission of an inability to make the production process respond to social goals to resort to taxation transfers as a substitute for income from factor payments.

On the other hand, the position hypothesized by Henry Simons (1938; 1948) that an enterprise economy tends to generate a distribution of income and wealth that is inconsistent with the continuation of political democracy seems particularly timely. The solution to this dilemma proposed by Simons, an effective system of progressive income taxation and transfers, is as relevant for our time as it was for his.

The "Crunch" and the Limitation to Aggregate Demand

The 1960s witnessed the apparent victory of Keynesian policy. However, the successful application of Keynesian policy may result in an economy that is inherently unstable. This instability is not the result of a tendency to stagnate or enter into a deep depression state; rather, it is due to a tendency to explode.

Between the end of World War II and the crunch of 1966, the American economy operated within an expectational climate in which decision makers were increasingly expecting reasonably full employment to be maintained and to an increasing extent both households and business were expecting next year to be better than this year. This trend in the expectational climate resulted in an explosively increasing demand for private investment in the mid-1960s.

Rising investment generates savings. During the 1950s, when a nascent investment boom took place, the savings took place as a result of changes in the federal government's budgetary position. This was due to the application of conventional fiscal precepts in designing tax and spending programs. In the 1960s, as a result of the

Effects of Shifts of Aggregate Demand upon Income Distribution
(1968)

combination of "modern" fiscal policy ideas and an accidental war, government revenues did not rise rapidly relative to government spending when private investment "exploded." Thus, the savings to offset the explosion of private investment had to come from the private sector.

The "Kaldorian" relation (Kaldor 1959), in which the propensity to save out of profits is greater than the propensity to save out of household disposable income, means that income distribution shifts toward profits whenever savings must be generated in the private sector. One way in which this change in the distribution of income can take place is through inflation. A rise of prices in excess of the rise in money wages lowers real wages. This classical inflation pattern, in which savings are forced by rising prices, was evident during 1966 and is an element in the continuing price pressure of 1967. Thus, not only does the "classical" (wages and profits) distribution of income "deteriorate" during an investment boom but also the deterioration is associated with a politically unpalatable inflation.

The contention that a measured 4 percent unemployment rate is full employment apparently was borne out by the accelerated rise in prices during 1966 and 1967. However, as wage increases were modest throughout most of 1966, the guidelines broke more on the price than the wage front; the mechanism of the inflation was not that of the Phillips curve (Phillips 1958).

Private investment lagged in the first three years of the current expansion and virtually exploded in the second three years. This investment explosion put serious pressures upon financial markets even in the absence of Federal Reserve action. When the Federal Reserve System applied some constraint, a "mini-panic" occurred.

The "mini-panic" of 1966 can be interpreted as evidence that sustained full employment may result in such an explosive increase in investment demand that it becomes impossible to achieve the sustained growth in demand necessary for continuing full employment. This is so because the investment boom is due to a "euphoric" expectational climate, and to break the investment boom it is necessary to change the expectational climate. Once the expectational climate is changed, all of the private sectors become sluggish.

Only by accident would public demand increase sufficiently quickly so that a relatively deep recession would not follow such a change in expectations. Of course, the deep depression ratifies the changed expectations and thus it will take time to rebuild confidence.

The destabilizing investment boom of the 1960s took place before unemployment rates were lowered to the levels which I characterized as tight full employment. If such explosive investment booms are a characteristic of American capitalism and they occur prematurely, then, in order to achieve and sustain tight full employment, it is necessary to contain the potential investment boom. One possible way is to so direct demand that it does not generate a large inducement to invest. Another possibility is to control investment directly, either by licensing investment or by licensing access to financial markets.

Impact of the Great Expansion upon Income Distribution

An important characteristic of the present-day American economy is the widespread belief, which has been validated by the overall performance of the economy since World War II, that next year will be better than this year. One way in which this "betterness" appears is in higher money incomes. Thus, the convention of annual "improvement" factors in union contracts. As long as a pattern of annual wage increases exists, changes in income distribution among wage earners will be due to the pattern of wage increases.

The evidence presented by Ulman (1965), mainly for post–World War II years prior to the recent expansion, is that a significant positive correlation exists between the original level of gross hourly earnings and the percentage change in gross hourly earnings. This contrasts with the finding for the depression and war years (Ross and Goldner 1950).

The pattern of arithmetic increases in wages that occurred during World War II translates into geometric increases that are inversely related to the original wage level, thus decreasing the range of relative earnings. During the early postwar period, the range changed but little. Between 1953 and 1960, the years of increasing overall slack in labor markets, the range widened. Between 1960 and 1966,

Effects of Shifts of Aggregate Demand upon Income Distribution
(1968)

the range of weekly wages has shown no real change, even though the dispersion of hourly rates as measured by the coefficient of variation has shown some narrowing over this recent expansion.

The initial observation for what follows is 1948. This year may be too close to the end of World War II, with its elaborate wage and price controls, to serve as a "model" for relative wages. Between 1953 and 1961, the trend was toward higher unemployment rates. The expansion of 1961–66 saw aggregate unemployment rates fall from 6.7 percent to 3.8 percent. Does chronic and growing labor market slack widen the range of weekly earnings among industries, whereas a period of labor market tightening or tightness narrows the spread?

Relative earnings in the 21 two-digit manufacturing industries plus mining, contract construction, wholesale trade, and retail trade were examined. For each year, the average weekly wage in each of the 25 sectors was divided by average earnings in all manufacturing to get relative wages.

In 1948, weekly earnings in four industries (Table 2.1) were in excess of 120 percent of the average earnings, and three industries exhibited earnings that were less than 80 percent of the base. In sharp contrast, in 1966, weekly earnings in six industries were in excess of 120 percent of all the manufacturing earnings, and earnings in six industries were below 80 percent of the base. Whereas in 1948, of the 25 industries, 18 were in the range "weekly earnings in all manufacturing ± 20 percent," in 1966 only 13 were in this range. (If "± 10 percent of all the manufacturing earnings" is used as the central group, 12 of the 25 industries were in the range in 1948, whereas only nine were in 1966.)

Not only has there been a marked thinning out of the middle of the range of weekly earnings by industry, but also the minimum average weekly income as a ratio to the average has decreased. In 1948, weekly earnings only in tobacco manufactures were below 70 percent of the average. In 1966, three industries exhibited weekly earnings lower than 70 percent of all manufacturing: these were leather and leather goods, apparel and related manufacturing, and retail trade.

Table 2.1 Ratio of Average Weekly Earnings to Average Weekly Earnings in All Manufacturing, 1948, 1953, 1960, 1966

Industry	1948	1953	1960	1966
Mining	1.234	1.178	1.175	1.158
Contract Construction	1.228	1.226	1.259	1.293
Ordnance and Accessories	1.078	1.108	1.208	1.209
Lumber and Wood Products	0.896	0.862	0.821	0.825
Furniture and Fixtures	0.919	0.893	0.838	0.813
Stone, Clay, and Glass Products	1.001	0.995	1.031	1.018
Primary Metal Industries	1.151	1.198	1.221	1.230
Fabricated Metal Products	1.060	1.085	1.096	1.084
Machinery	1.136	1.173	1.165	1.202
Electrical Equipment	1.026	1.000	1.011	0.969
Transportation Equipment	1.162	1.210	1.242	1.267
Instruments and Related Products	0.989	1.030	1.040	1.010
Miscellaneous Manufacturing	0.904	0.873	0.827	0.791
Food and Kindred Products	0.920	0.901	0.959	0.925
Tobacco Manufactures	0.689	0.675	0.723	0.758
Textile Mill Products	0.822	0.754	0.708	0.731
Apparel and Allied Products	0.822	0.691	0.627	0.613
Paper and Related Products	1.030	1.019	1.060	1.063
Printing and Publishing	1.226	1.167	1.147	1.092
Chemicals and Allied Products	1.041	1.053	1.150	1.118
Petroleum and Related Products	1.304	1.282	1.322	1.288
Rubber and Plastic Products	1.004	1.031	1.031	0.995
Leather and Leather Products	0.773	0.722	0.674	0.667
Wholesale Trade	1.009	0.978	1.011	0.990
Retail Trade	0.784	0.705	0.695	0.611

Source: Department of Labor (1968), Table C-6: Gross Average Weekly Earnings of Production or Non-Supervisory Workers on Payrolls of Selected Industries Annual Averages

Effects of Shifts of Aggregate Demand upon Income Distribution
(1968)

Of the 10 industries with the highest weekly earnings in 1948, seven had increased their relative earnings by 1966, one exhibited no serious change, and two (mining, and printing and publishing) had suffered substantial relative declines.

Of the eight industries with the lowest relative wages in 1948, seven had experienced a substantial decline in their relative wages by 1966. The exception, tobacco, had the lowest average weekly earnings in 1948 (69 percent of the all manufacturing average earnings). By 1966, this ratio for tobacco was 76 percent, and tobacco manufactures were fifth from the bottom in weekly earnings.

Some of the declines in relative weekly earnings were really substantial. Earnings in apparel fell from 82 percent to 61 percent of the average of all manufacturing, furniture from 92 to 81 percent, leather from 78 to 67 percent, textiles from 82 to 73 percent, and lumber from 90 to 83 percent. In addition, retail trade fell from 78 to 61 percent and miscellaneous manufactures from 90 to 79 percent.

The seven industries that ranked from 11th (paper and allied products, relative earnings 103 percent) to 17th (food, relative earnings 92 percent) in 1948 tended to show but slight changes in their relative earnings in the period to 1966. The relative earnings of electrical equipment dropped 6 percent; all the others remained approximately unchanged in relative earnings: that is, the terminal-year relative earning was ± 3 percent of the initial relative earnings.

Thus, over the period 1948–66, for the industries examined, the rich tended to get richer, the poor tended to get poorer, and those in the middle tended to hold their own.

If 1948–66 is broken into three subperiods, 1948–53, 1953–60, and 1960–66, the spreading of relative weekly earnings and the thinning out of the middle range occurred during each period, although it has occurred at an accelerated rate since 1953. Whereas weekly earnings in 18 industries in 1948 were in the middle range (80 percent to 119 percent of the average in all manufacturing), 17 industries in 1953, 15 industries in 1960, and 13 industries in 1966 were in this range (Table 2.2).

The increase in the spread since 1948 seems to be mainly due to the relative retardation in the increase in earnings in what were

Table 2.2 Average Weekly Earnings in 21 Manufacturing Industries, Mining, Construction, and Trade: Distribution of Relative Wages (all manufacturing = 100), 1948, 1953, 1960, 1966

Weekly Wage as a Percentage of All Manufacturing	Number of Industries			
	1948	1953	1960	1966
120.0 and above	4	3	5	6
110.0–119.9	3	5	4	2
110.00–109.9	8	6	7	5
90.0–99.9	4	3	1	4
80.0–89.9	3	3	3	2
70.0–79.9	2	3	2	3
69.9 or less	1	2	3	3

Source: Table 2.1

already low-wage industries. The relative retardation of what were two high-earning industries in 1948—mining, and printing and publishing—is perhaps mainly due to technological changes, although the relative retardation of earnings in mining is a part of today's rural poverty scene.

Many of the industries in which relative wages declined between 1948 and 1966 were "sick" for part or all of this period. In the case of the textile, apparel, leather, and furniture industries, one response to difficulties was a rather large-scale migration from major metropolitan centers and their historical areas toward small towns and the South.

A theorem seems to fall out of the experience of the postwar period. Marked declines in relative wage earnings in an industry will be accompanied by changes in the location of the plants in the industry.

The maintenance, or even a continuation of the thinning-out trend, during the expansion of 1961–66 is evidence that the supply curves of labor to the industries with low relative wages remained highly elastic as the overall unemployment rate decreased. This may reflect their locational advantages: with rural areas as a continuing source of labor, the advantageously located low-wage industries may in fact be operating with a huge reservoir of labor, responsive to job opportunities at unchanging markups over rural incomes.

As measured by the coefficient of variation, the spread of hourly earnings decreased slightly between 1960 and 1966, after increasing in 1948–53 and 1953–60. In spite of this, the coefficient of variation for weekly earnings increased between 1960 and 1966. Thus, hours worked were positively correlated with earnings so that the distribution of weekly earnings had a wider range than the distribution of hourly earnings. Inasmuch as it is earnings over a period, not the hourly rate, that is important in income distribution, the minor drawing together of hourly rates that occurred during the expansion is not especially significant.

Leading Sectors in Generating Aggregate Demand and Income Distribution

Aggregate demand has a structure which, in turn, generates the particular (including regional) demands for products and factors. The government impact upon aggregate demand also has a structure. As long as income distribution is a "minor" or, better, an "unmentionable" policy goal, then the impact upon income distribution of the particular structure of government programs can be ignored. Once the achievement of some maximum inequality becomes a recognized social imperative, then the way in which government affects income distribution becomes a factor in policy decisions.

A number of factors have combined to create the "shortages in the midst of surpluses" labor markets of the past 10 to 15 years, and the resultant spreading of relative incomes. One has been the peculiar pattern of government demand. It is only necessary to note how government spending on research and development has grown and to combine this with the growth of spending on education to recognize that leading sectors, in terms of the growth of aggregate demand, have generated initial demand for highly skilled professional and technical labor. Even though to a large extent the impact of government has been of a stop-go nature, the research-plus-education growth has been fairly steady.

A second factor in determining the changes in relative incomes has been the rapid migration from rural areas, in particular the movement of Negroes from the rural South (Perkins and Hathaway 1966). This has generated a large—nay, an infinitely elastic—supply of unskilled and semiskilled workers in the cities. The disturbing results reported by Batchelder (1964), that Negro male incomes deteriorated relative to white male incomes between 1950 and 1960 within the relevant cells indicates that the data on average wages by industry may obscure increasing spreads of incomes within each industry.

A third factor tending to spread relative earnings has been the stop-go nature of many facets of the economy since World War II. Over this period, on the whole, the American economy has done well. However, this overall "smoothness" has been the result of a series of stop-go developments in various sectors. Not only has the country engaged in two "minor" wars, but also the leading sectors have shifted with great rapidity from general defense, to missiles, to space, to private investment. Each time a new government program, be it highways or aid to education or moon shots, gets under way, local excess demand for labor is generated.

The impact of new leading sectors upon wages is different from a rise in employment that takes the form of rehiring previously employed workers, and from the expansion of conventional industries. Whenever local demand for labor exceeds supply, wages rise (Lipsey 1960, Schultze 1960). In addition, wage increases in a sector spill over to other sectors, even in the face of overall labor market slack. This is so because productivity of labor is a function of "morale," and a decline in relative wages adversely affects morale. However, in the presence of slack, wage increases in the following sectors will be lower than in the leading sectors.

If a series of stop-go shocks occurs, and if these shocks all have their major initial labor market impact upon a restricted set of labor markets, then the wage in this restricted set will rise relative to others. If these repeated impacts occur upon what are already high-wage industries and occupations, then the distribution of income will be adversely affected.

Effects of Shifts of Aggregate Demand upon Income Distribution
(1968)

A test of whether the pattern of aggregate–demand creation has affected the distribution of income, by a succession of such impacts upon the demand for particular classes of workers, is needed. Detailed occupational income data and a way of transforming each period's leading sector into demand for labor in particular categories are required for such a test.

Policy Suggestions

From the above, I extract two propositions relevant to policy formation:

1. The American economy as presently organized is not capable of achieving and sustaining tight full employment.
2. Within the employment limitations of the economy, there is no significant tendency toward a narrowing of the spread of relative income from labor.

I add to the above that a narrowing of the spread of income from labor is necessary.

If the post–World War II pattern of shifting leading sectors determining aggregate demand leads to perverse changes in the distribution of income, then we ought to consider changing the pattern of leading sectors. A suggestion of real merit is that the government become an employer of last resort.

One attribute of such a "tap" employer is that, when the terms upon which it will employ are set, the minimum wage for all is determined. There is no longer any question about the "coverage" of minimum-wage legislation. In addition, the minimum wage set in this manner does not have an adverse effect upon employment, as may be true for the present minimum-wage legislation. The relative size of the wage set by the employer of last resort determines the division of the labor force between the private and the public sectors.

In a world where nominal wages are expected to increase each year, some improvement factor needs to be included in the terms upon which the employer of last resort hires. If the improvement factor for the employer of last resort rises at a faster rate than average and above-average wages, the range of relative wages decreases. In time, if such differential rates of change are sustained, a target ratio between the minimum and average can be achieved.

To the extent that the high-wage worker's nominal income rises at some "productivity rate," the low-wage worker's nominal income will need to rise at some faster rate: there may be an inflationary bias in an incomes policy that takes as one of its imperatives the achievement of greater equality. In addition, it will be necessary to restrain profits and investment; in particular, the highly destabilizing tendency for investment demand to explode will have to be brought under control.

Although we currently view the crisis in income distribution as centering around the urban ghettos, much of poverty is rural. An employer of last resort, willing and able to hire all who offer to work, will have a large impact on the poorer rural areas. One effect of such a national employment policy will be to slow down the pace of migration to the urban complexes. Inasmuch as many of the urban problems are related to the rapid rate of migration, such a retaining effect following from an employer of last resort will be an added virtue.

Much experimentation with tap employment policies—and its equivalent, the creation of programs which will have their major initial impact upon present unemployed labor—will be needed. However, the objective is clear: it is to take the labor force as it is and make sure that fitting jobs are available. Instead of the demand for the low-wage worker trickling down from the demand for the high-wage worker, such a policy should result in increments of demand for present high-wage workers "bubbling up" from the demand for low-wage workers.

Effects of Shifts of Aggregate Demand upon Income Distribution (1968)

Sources

Anderson, W. H. L. 1964. "Trickling Down: The Relationship between Economic Growth and the Extent of Poverty among American Families." *Quarterly Journal of Economics* 78(4): 511–24.

Batchelder, A. B. 1964. "Decline in the Relative Income of Negro Men." *Quarterly Journal of Economics* 78(4): 525–48.

Department of Labor. 1967. *Manpower Report of the President*. Washington, D.C.: Government Printing Office.

Green, C. 1967. *Negative Taxes and the Poverty Problem*. Washington, D.C.: The Brookings Institution.

Kaldor, N. 1959. "Economic Growth and the Problem of Inflation, Part I." *Economica* 26(104): 287–98.

Lipsey, R. G. 1960. "The Relation between Unemployment and the Rate of Change of Money Wage Rates in the United Kingdom, 1862–1957: A Further Analysis." *Economica* 27(105): 1–31.

Minsky, H. P. 1965. "The Role of Employment Policy." In Margaret S. Gordon, ed. *Poverty in America*. Proceedings of a national conference held at the University of California, Berkeley, February 26–28, 1965. San Francisco: Chandler Publishing Company, 175–200. Reprinted as chapter 1 in the present volume.

Perkins, B., and D. Hathaway. 1966. "The Movement of Labor between Farm and Non-Farm Jobs." Research Bulletin 13. Michigan State University, Agricultural Experiment Station.

Phillips, A. W. 1958. "The Relation between Unemployment and the Rate of Change of Money Wage Rates in the United Kingdom, 1861–1957." *Economica* 25(100): 283–99.

Ross, A. M., and W. Goldner. 1950. "Forces Affecting the Interindustry Wage Structure." *Quarterly Journal of Economics* 64(2): 254–81.

Schultze, C. L. 1960. "Recent Inflation in the United States." Study Paper No. 1. In *Employment, Growth and Price Levels*. Report of the Joint Economic Committee, pursuant to Senate Concurrent Resolution 13, 86th Cong., 1st sess. S. Rep. No. 1043 (January).

Scitovsky, T. 1964. "Equity." In *Papers on Welfare and Growth*. Palo Alto, Calif.: Stanford University Press.

Simons, H. C. 1938. *Personal Income Taxation: The Definition of Income as a Problem of Fiscal Policy*. Chicago: University of Chicago Press.

———. 1948. "A Positive Program for Laissez-Faire: Some Proposals for a Liberal Economic Policy." In *Economic Policy for a Free Society*, 40–77. Chicago: University of Chicago Press.

Ulman, L. 1965. "Labor Mobility and the Industrial Wage Structure in the Postwar United States." *Quarterly Journal of Economics* 79(1): 73–97.

Chapter 3

Policy and Poverty* (1969)

Introduction

In a rich country, poverty is a matter of income distribution. This is true whether one measures poverty in an absolute or a relative sense. Poverty in the sense of relative deprivation is a matter of the shape of the distribution of income: no matter how high the absolute income, those with incomes much below the average are adjudged poor. Thus, in a rich country, public policy aimed to eradicate poverty can take the form of programs designed to truncate the lower tail of the distribution of income so that very few are far below some average, an average which, for countries afflicted with relative poverty, is acknowledged to yield an adequate level of living.

Before we proceed it is best to make precise the definition of income that seems to be appropriate for a discussion of relative deprivation poverty. Almost all of those classed as poor in a rich country enjoy a private disposable income (earned income minus direct taxes plus transfer payments) sufficient to maintain life at a standard far above that which all but a tiny minority achieve in countries such as India and Pakistan, where absolute poverty is the lot of almost all. Part of the poverty problem in the United States centers around the social and personal reaction to how income is received. The welfare recipient can be poor, even if welfare standards are adequate, if cash income derived from welfare is personally and socially demeaning. Thus social dividend or negative income tax proposals which seemingly remove such stigmas have a receptive audience.

It follows that poverty in the United States relates to the subjective evaluation of well-being, what economists have called utility, as much as to the size distribution of conventionally defined income. The relevant income for the study of poverty would measure the total satisfaction, adjusted for purely personal events, that a

---

* "Policy and Poverty, Part 1"; "Policy and Poverty, Part 2"; "Policy and Poverty, Part 3." Draft manuscript. Papers 8, 9, 10. Hyman P. Minsky Archive, Levy Economics Institute, Annandale-on-Hudson, N.Y.

household gets from both privately procured and publicly provided goods and services. Note that a job in and of itself may be an ingredient in income thought of in this manner.

Such a "satisfaction income" concept can also encompass a horizon that extends over several generations, so that economic opportunity, in the sense of an expected higher income and status for children, becomes a part of present income. In an open society, if the typical horizon is long, the relevant income of the current ambitious and confident poor can be substantially higher than their measured income.

This satisfaction income concept, like utility, cannot be measured directly. A proxy for this income concept might be some measure of the view of the purely relative poor about the fairness or equity of the economy. Thus the existence of a consensus about equity joins efficiency, growth, and stability as a criterion for judging an economy and as a goal of public policy (Scitovsky 1964).

Relative deprivation poverty, in contrast to absolute poverty, is truly a many-faceted beast. A thorough study of such poverty as a public policy problem primarily dealing with the distribution of income involves measuring the differential social impacts of various measures that could be taken to affect the distribution of measured income. This is beyond my competence, and, I believe, beyond the present state of the arts in the relevant social disciplines. Thus, even though the social impact of policies designed to affect the distribution of income may be more significant in determining views about dimensions such as equity than changes in the distribution of private disposable income plus public goods, the emphasis in this paper will be on measures that could be undertaken in order to achieve a more equal distribution of private disposable income as well as to increase the publicly supplied goods.

In designing public policies to affect income distribution it is necessary to keep in mind that "there are some economic forces so powerful that they constantly break through all barriers erected for their suppression" (Baumol 1967). However, economics after Keynes is not a dismal science. To a modern economist the constraining powerful economic forces do not so restrict what can be

Policy and Poverty (1969)

so that what exists must be accepted as inevitable. But as Baumol reminds us, the possibility of policy does not mean that a "good" idea will necessarily achieve a desired goal.

Economic forces can frustrate programs if either the policy objective is inconsistent with such forces or the program is so poorly conceived that it quite unnecessarily runs afoul of a barrier, even though the objective is, in principle, attainable. Thus an essential step in designing programs is to determine whether forces exist which would make a program ineffective, and whether a particular policy goal is in fact impossible to achieve — perhaps given some set of nonnegotiable institutional characteristics — or whether the difficulty arises because the policy instruments that are being proposed are not efficient. Such analysis should make it possible to select programs that get around barriers that are due to the policy instruments used and abort attempts to achieve impossible goals. In addition, if a "nonnegotiable" institutional constraint is an effective barrier to the achievement of a policy goal, the radical question of the value of such institutions needs to be faced.

This paper will take up some [of the] economic forces that can frustrate programs to end or alleviate poverty. However, to the extent that inflation, for example, is a result of policies designed to eliminate poverty, the political response to inflation and whether or not inflation is equitable among classes becomes important. Thus what is attempted here can be extended by investigating the social, cultural, and political forces that also cannot be suppressed, excepting, perhaps, at a large cost.

In this paper I will first sketch a feasible program of radical changes in the distribution of income by biasing the distribution of the increments to income and then examine a number of barriers which must be taken into account in designing policies to eliminate poverty or redistribute income in the United States. This will be followed by some suggestions for a policy strategy which hopefully gets around the listed barriers. The barriers which will be taken up deal with:

1) the macroeconomics of the negative income tax*,
2) the limitations upon economic growth,
3) the stability of relative wages, and
4) the feedbacks from sustained full employment.

I doubt if my list is exhaustive.

The major conclusion of the paper is that an effective program of income equalization or poverty elimination will need to be linked to the production of output, which can take the form of public goods. Instead of transfers by taxation, which will not work, a program of expansion of public employment and public sector output might do the job. One reason is that, potentially, the poor could receive a large portion of their income in public goods; the second reason is that such a program could add many of the present poor to the public payrolls. It is necessary in designing such a program that the well-off, who are, so to say, being discriminated against, receive recognizable benefits from the income equalization program.

One obvious barrier to the elimination of poverty that will not be discussed is due to the existence of a military establishment whose fun and games absorb some 10 percent of the GNP. This is an especially relevant barrier to the elimination of poverty, for income used here includes the perceived benefits from the output of the public sectors. We can assume that for many Americans the perceived benefits from foreign adventures, military procurement, and space spectaculars are less, per dollar of expenditure, than from private procurement and public goods such as schools, parks, and safety on the streets. This barrier will not be discussed in detail because I assume, perhaps heroically, that it does not reflect powerful forces inherent in the American enterprise economy. No matter how powerful the military-industrial research institute complex may be, they are not, I hope, an essential characteristic of American capitalism.

Underlying this paper is the view that good intentions, bright slogans, and cadres of happy warriors are not enough. Programs must be consistent with the nature of the beast; the behavioral rules

---

* The topic is not taken up in the "Policy and Poverty" manuscripts. It is dealt with in chapter 4 of the present volume, which Minsky wrote separately.

of the economy determine whether programs can possibly have the intended effect. Policy programs not designed to avoid or not powerful enough to overcome such economic barriers will clearly be counterproductive. Hopes raised then dashed are a clear danger to the fabric of society. Every policy failure becomes evidence to those who do not accept the policy goal that, in fact, it is impossible [to realize]. The capabilities of our economy to generate a viable and desirable social order have not been tested, and they will not be tested unless the implications of programs designed to achieve policy goals are thought through before they are implemented.

The Arithmetic of Radical Income Equalization

During the Great Depression, Huey Long articulated radical income equalization ideals with his slogans "Share the Wealth" and "Every Man a King." The call to share what in principle already existed reflected the stagnationist view of the economy which for obvious reasons was then dominant. In an optimistic era such as the recent past, when the arithmetic of compound interest inspired the prevalent view of normal functioning of the [economy], income equalization or the elimination of poverty could be visualized as being achieved by biasing, in favor of the poor, the distribution of the increments of income due to economic growth.

In the 1969 *Economic Report of the President*, the Council of Economic Advisers wrote, "Only a relatively small redistribution of the benefits of growth is needed to speed greatly the reduction in poverty.... If the increase in real income for the nonpoor is lowered merely from 3 percent to 2.5 percent a year and if that differential of about $2.8 billion annually is effectively transferred to those in poverty, then family incomes for those now poor can grow about 12 percent annually. This redistribution would eliminate the 1967 'poverty gap' of $9.7 billion in less than 4 years. Since any program of redistribution would be likely to reach some of the near-poor and might raise some poor families substantially above the poverty line before others are affected, perhaps a better projection of the time required would be 6 to 8 years" (CEA 1969, 160).

There is no doubt that the modest result envisaged by the Council is arithmetically feasible. The body of this section consists of an arithmetic example of what is involved in biasing the distribution of the growth in income so as to achieve income equalization or the elimination of official poverty within a designated period. The possible variations in programs with the broad objectives of income redistribution are infinite. Two principles underlie the program presented. These are that the portion of the population being discriminated against (the better-off) should nevertheless enjoy some improvement in their living standard during each period, and that the period during which the distribution of the benefits from growth is biased toward the poor should be rather short. In addition to these principles, it is necessary to decide for exactly how long the program should be in effect, the target group, and the distributive objective of the income equalization program before a specific program can be spelled out. The period chosen for the example is a decade, and the target is a radical equalization program designed to place a large proportion of the total population close to the present day's median income, adjusted for economic growth over the decade.

The radical income equalization objective turns out to be almost inconsistent with the principle that the well-off should continue to benefit at an appreciable rate throughout the program. It is shown that the sacrifice of growth of income by the well-off increases as time elapses; this would be true of a more modest program as well.

However, the difficulties with any radical income equalization program lie in the economics, not in the arithmetic. Assuming the validity of the projected growth in income and population, many different feasible programs can be constructed. The deep question is whether there exists any economic mechanism by which the arithmetically possible goals can be achieved.

In the optimistic mid-1960s, "fiscal dividend" was a popular phrase. It referred to the rise in government receipts that would accompany a growth in income with tax schedules unchanged. The fiscal dividend was supposed to make both a rise in government spending and a lowering of the tax schedule possible. For example, a rather generous children's allowance of some $25 a month for all children through 14 years of age would cost in the neighborhood of two years' fiscal dividend. Thus, in a "growthman's" world, it is only necessary for a transfer scheme to cost less than the growth in the government's tax take with fixed schedules for it to involve no rise and even to allow for a reduction in tax schedules. If a transfer scheme involves transfers in excess of the increment of the tax take with a fixed schedule but less than the rise in income, then even though the tax schedule would have to be raised, it would still be possible for all to enjoy a rise in income. Only if a transfer scheme involves transfers greater than the rise in income would it necessarily require a decline in income for some.

In the above paragraphs the technique for achieving radical income equalization is identified with some unspecified transfer scheme. These could take the form of a negative income tax, wage supplements, or some set of specific programs such as child allowances and old-age pensions. Transfer payments need not carry the entire burden of income equalization if sharp changes in relative incomes from work can be effected or if public employment is undertaken.

Income is defined here as personal income. Thus the income concept is narrower than that which was deemed most appropriate for the study of poverty, which is disposable income plus income in kind from public goods.

Rainwater[*] has called for a nation of average men. This is interpreted here as the existence of an income distribution in which approximately 50 percent of the family units are in a narrow lowest-income class, with the incomes of the other 50 percent of the population distributed as in the upper tail of the present income distribution. In Rainwater's idea this narrow lowest class is to be centered around the present median income.

In 1966, the median income was about $7,400, i.e., it was in the $7,000–7,999 income class. The income equalization target that was selected for the arithmetic exercise was to bring all incomes below the median class up to an $8,000 level in 1976, and to allow all incomes in the median income class and above to increase at a

---

[*] Lee Rainwater.

growth rate [consistent] with this income equalization objective and the postulated rate of growth in aggregate income.

The arithmetic example assumes a 4 percent growth rate of real GNP and a 1.25 percent growth rate of population. Thus a 2.75 percent growth rate in per capita income was assumed. On the basis of the most recent observations, the growth rate assumed for real GNP may be a bit small, and the growth rate assumed for population may be somewhat high. If this is so, then, as the income to be redistributed is fixed in per capita terms by the redistribution goals, the income available for increasing the real per capita income of the upper income groups will be greater than assumed. Thus the virtual stagnation of the above-median per capita income toward the end of the program decade will not be necessary.[1]

For every income class below the $7,000 level, the ratio of $8,000 to the midpoint of the income class was calculated. From this, the rate of growth which, if compounded over a decade, would transform the class midpoint income into the target income can be determined. Thus $8,000 ÷ $2,250 = 3.56, and a 13.5 percent annual rate of growth of real income will transform the income of the midpoint of this income class into $8,000. (See Table 3.1 for the required growth rates for all income classes.)

The burden of such an income equalization program increases with time. In the first year of such a program some $2.96 billion would be redistributed; this is but 17.9 percent of the $16.52 billion rise in income during the year. In the 10th year (1976 in the example) family income will have grown by $198.4 billion, but in this, the final year of the program, the total cost of redistribution will be $68 billion; 34.2 percent of the decade's increase in income will have gone into the redistribution pot. As a result of this increased burden of the redistribution program, the rate of growth of per capita income of the upper-income group decreases from 1.89 percent in the first year to 0.19 percent in the 10th year.

It seems obvious that the program detailed here, though arithmetically feasible, might be politically unpalatable. A redistribution program must yield "benefits" to all, and a rise in per capita income of the just-above-middle groups by 0.19 percent while rapid advances of the impoverished are taking place seems politically indigestible. It also seems obvious that there is not enough income in one half of 1 percent of income, the redistribution postulated by the President's Council, to effect a radical equalization of income in a finite time; the ratio of the increment in redistribution to the increment of income growth is 54.4 percent in the 10th year. This means that some 2.1 percent of the overall income in the terminal year would have to be distributed via some scheme from the upper-income to the lower-income groups.

A more modest target or one stretched over more years will be arithmetically feasible and might also be more attractive politically. Thus, if the original program is sustained for seven years, the upper income groups would still be enjoying in excess of 1 percent increase in per capita income in the terminal year. Over the seven-year time interval, the bottom $500 group would have risen to about $3,000 and the group with a midpoint of $1,250 per year would have risen to about $4,560. The $4,500 midpoint-class income would have risen by some 31 percent to about $6,000. That is, the radical program might be adopted for a shorter time, leaving the final approach to the Rainwater goal for a longer stretch of time.

It is a characteristic of the algebra of geometric processes of redistribution that the burden of the program grows and is greatest in its final stages. Thus growing political objections to redistribution programs can be expected as they progress unless the programs of redistribution simultaneously yield benefits, perhaps in kind, to the already well-off. A transfer-by-taxation scheme (negative income taxes) might not be politically acceptable even for a modest goal, whereas a work program with the same income equalization results that yields perceived benefits to the upper income groups might be acceptable. A program for radical income equalization cannot be accepted as the basis for action just because the arithmetic checks out.

The Limitation on Economic Growth

An arithmetically feasible program of radical income equalization depends critically upon the rate of growth of aggregate output.

Table 3.1 Distribution of Family Income, 1966

Total Money Income	Percentage of Families — Per Interval	Percentage of Families — Cumulative	Percentage of Family Income — Per Interval	Percentage of Family Income — Cumulative	Annual Growth Rate Necessary to Achieve Objectives Indicated (in percent)
Under 1,000	2.3	2.3	.14	.14	32.0
1,000–1,499	2.3	4.6	.34	.48	20.4
1,500–1,999	3.1	7.7	.64	1.12	16.4
2,000–2,499	3.4	11.1	.91	2.03	13.5
2,500–2,999	3.2	14.3	1.04	3.07	11.3
3,000–3,499	3.5	17.8	1.35	4.42	9.4
3,500–3,999	3.3	21.1	1.47	5.89	7.9
4,000–4,999	7.1	28.2	3.78	9.67	5.9
5,000–5,999	8.4	36.6	5.47	15.14	3.8
6,000–6,999	9.47	46.0	7.10	22.34	2.1
7,000–7,999	9.3	55.3	8.25	30.59	*
8,000–8,999	8.1	63.4	8.15	38.74	*
9,000–9,999	7.0	70.4	7.88	46.62	*
10,000–11,999	11.2	81.6	14.59	61.21	*
12,000–14,999	9.2	90.8	14.71	75.92	*
15,000–24,999	7.5	98.3	16.87	92.79	*
Over 25,000	1.7	100.0	7.22	100.00	*

* See Table 3.2.

Table 3.2 Hypothetical Income Equalization Program, 1967–76

Year	Rate of Growth of Per Capita Income in "Upper Income Groups" (in percent)	Growth of Family Income since 1966 (in billions of dollars) During Year	Growth of Family Income since 1966 (in billions of dollars) Total	Cost of Redistribution (in billions of dollars) Total	Cost of Redistribution (in billions of dollars) Increment during Year	Cost of Redistribution / Growth of Family Income (in percent) Total since 1966	Cost of Redistribution / Growth of Family Income (in percent) Increment during Year
1967	1.89	16.52	16.52	2.96	2.96	17.9	17.9
1968	1.79	17.19	33.71	6.45	3.49		
1969	1.69	17.87	51.58	10.53	4.08		
1970	1.57	18.58	70.16	15.31	4.78		
1971	1.43	19.34	89.50	20.92	5.61	TO BE COMPUTED	
1972	1.26	20.11	109.61	27.52	6.60		
1973	1.06	20.90	130.51	35.27	7.75		
1974	0.82	21.75	152.26	44.41	9.14		
1975	0.54	22.61	174.87	55.20	10.79		
1976	0.19	23.52	198.39	68.00	12.80	34.2	54.4

Ed. Note: This table is a draft and remains incomplete.

If output does not grow fast enough, then the path to income equalization, or even the path to a much more modest goal, the elimination of poverty, can be blocked.

There are factors which can reduce the rate of growth of output, even if full employment is maintained. To a large extent the growth in overall output per capita has been the result of differing rates of growth in productivity in the various sectors.[2] If the output of sectors with high or rapidly increasing labor productivity is growing fast enough, so that their total employment increases, then total output will tend to grow rapidly. If the output of such sectors is growing slowly, so that the labor force in these sectors is declining, then overall growth in output will be slowed.

Thus, in our model, rapid growth is compounded of two elements—rapid rates of increase in productivity in some sectors and increases in employment in these progressive sectors. If factors are operative which tend to rapidly increase the labor force allocated to sectors where productivity grows slowly, then the rate of growth of output would tend to decline. It may very well be that the current need for improvement in the urban service sectors is such a growth-reducing factor.

Baumol (1967) has made precise, within a simple two-sector growth model, some of the implications of unbalanced growth in productivity. He postulates the existence of two sectors—one technologically progressive, the other technologically stagnant. In the progressive sector, output per standard laborer grows exponentially. In the stagnant sector, output per standard laborer remains constant. For the growth of income and the movements of the price level to be determined, it is necessary to make precise assumptions about the assignment of labor and relative wages in the two sectors.

The Baumol model consists of two sectors, a stagnant sector in which labor productivity does not grow at all and a progressive sector in which productivity grows at a constant exponential rate given by e^{rt}. Thus, in the stagnant sector

(1) $Y_{st} = aL_{st}$ and in the progressive sector

(2) $Y_{pt} = bL_{pt}e^{rt}$. In addition, wages grow at the same rate as productivity in the progressive sector,

Policy and Poverty (1969)

(3) $W_t = W_o e^{rt}$. The wage behavior assumption is not necessary, excepting that it enables us to make precise statements about the behavior of the price level.

The implications of these assumptions can be stated in four theorems (Baumol 1967, 417–19).

Theorem 1. The cost per unit of output in the stagnant sector C_s will rise without limit, while C_p, the unit cost in one progressive sector, will remain constant.

[. . .]*

Theorem 2. There is a tendency for the outputs of the stagnant sectors whose demands are not highly inelastic with respect to price or elastic enough with respect to income to decline and perhaps, ultimately, to vanish.

[. . .]

Theorem 3. If the ratio of the output of the two sectors is held constant, more and more of the labor force must be allocated to the stagnant sector and the amount of labor in the progressive sector will tend to approach zero.

Corollary. If the labor force is growing, a larger and larger percentage of the labor force will be assigned to the stagnant sector.

[. . .]

Theorem 4. An attempt to achieve balanced growth in a world of unbalanced productivity must lead to a declining rate of growth relative to the growth in the labor force. In particular, if productivity in one sector and the total labor force remain constant, the growth rate of the economy will asymptotically approach zero.

[. . .]

Corollary. If balanced growth is sustained in a world of unbalanced technology and money wages rise at the rate of increase of productivity in the progressive sector, then the rate of increase of prices will approach the rate of increase of productivity.

[. . .]

If the technologically progressive sector is commodity production and the technologically stagnant sector is the service and,

---

* Ellipses that follow indicate location of handwritten equations in manuscript (borrowed from Baumol [1967]). Removed here for readability.

particularly, the government sector, then the Baumol model has a certain charm as a tool for interpreting current problems and recent history. The early postwar period witnessed a veritable explosion in commodity production, and the income and price elasticities of demand were such that a relative growth of commodity production took place, to the neglect of the publicly supplied amenities and services. The starving of the public sector under the conditions of the 1950s was one of the themes of Galbraith's* *Affluent Society*—a volume which also announced the elimination of all but pocket- and casebook poverty.

The easy identification of services with low productivity growth and commodities with high productivity growth should not be carried too far. In the process sketched in the theorems, a relative price ratio can develop at which the mechanization of service production becomes feasible. The development and proliferation of car-washing machines and the coming substitution of the labor-economizing telephonic facsimile printer for the mailed letter are examples. The relative rise in the cost of postal services, particularly the impossibility of substituting machines for the human reader of human scrawls, implies that in the not-too-distant future the facsimile transmission of personal mail over telephonic wires will be cheaper than the present mail system in urban centers.

The wiring of our households with facsimile receivers and transmitters, newspaper printing devices, and wired television is already feasible—and would increase labor productivity in what now seems like a set of chronically stagnant sectors.

Thus the labor assigned to income elastic–price inelastic technologically stagnant sectors of the economy may grow, but the rise in relative prices, the ever-rising portion of GNP spent on these sectors will act as a lure to the introduction of new techniques. This implies that whenever the production of a labor-intensive, apparently income-elastic, commodity or service draws an increasing volume of employment, there exists a real challenge in terms of the potential payoff from particular technological changes. Thus job

---

* John Kenneth Galbraith.

elimination, reminiscent of the substitution of automatic for manual elevators, can be expected to occur.

The message is that the process sketched by Baumol does change relative prices and tends to drive certain productions, especially those that are not especially income elastic or price inelastic, out of the market. For the income-elastic and price-inelastic stagnant sectors, the growth of employment and income produced in the sector serves as a lure for technical progress. Thus the drag on growth and the stimulus to accelerated increases in price levels from Baumol's disease should not be viewed as a necessarily permanent affair but rather as a recurrent "stage" which leads to cycles in the growth of an economy.

Baumol's model shows us that there is a lure to technical progress in changing relative prices and to factor allocations, but there is no guarantee that the progress will occur. First, there may be temporary—or even long-run—blocks due to knowledge and engineering problems.

Education and perhaps some aspects of police work (which may be one aspect of education under consideration, i.e., custodial care of children) seem to require a fixed high-labor input per unit of output. The custodial aspect of hospital care—bedpans and alcohol rubs—remains labor intensive, and the sophisticated aspects of medical care are also labor intensive. Thus there will at any time be a core of labor-intensive, price-inelastic, income-elastic services which will be the essential drag on output growth.

In addition, there will at any time be bureaucratic or institutional blocks to technical progress. The railways, public mass transportation, and the postal system are three examples that readily come to mind where the vested interests of labor and management combine to continue traditional ways of doing things. At present, the vested interests of the over-the-air broadcasters and the regulating authority are standing in the way of progress in the direction of the "wired city," which, in combination with facsimile transmission and electronic printers, will be the solution to the labor-intensive distribution of much of the printed matter.

The relative size and the relevant elasticities of output of the technologically and institutionally recalcitrant sectors will determine the rate of growth of the economy. At some periods the stagnant sectors—because of a recent breakthrough—will be relatively small, so that the rate of growth of real GNP will be high. At other times they will be large, so that the rate of growth of real GNP will be small.

With the rate of growth of GNP a variable depending upon technological and institutional time-dependent variables, the viability of a trickle-down or share-the-growth policy philosophy toward poverty is also variable. In periods when GNP grows rapidly, even a small bias in the distribution of income in [favor] of the lower-income population can result in a sharp rise in their income. For example, if the top 20 percent have 50 percent of the aggregate income and the bottom 20 percent have 5 percent of the income, a shift of 1 percent of the top 20 percent's income to the bottom 20 percent of the population can result in a 10 percent growth in the income of the bottom 20 percent. If GNP per capita is growing, say, at 5 percent per year, then the income of the top group can grow at 4 percent while the income of the bottom group can grow at 15 percent. If growth in per capita income slows to 1 percent per year, then by holding the top group fixed an 11 percent growth in the income of the bottom group can be achieved. In an environment where the median income group's growth in income is restricted to 1 percent a year, any attempt to redistribute in favor of the bottom group will be associated with considerable social friction.

As an aside—and the slowdown in income growth of the median income groups was mainly due to factors associated with the war in Vietnam rather than those identified as Baumol's disease—the Wallace* phenomena and the more active resistance to Negro demands occurred during a period in which the real income of the industrial wage earner may have been stagnant due to inflation. If the blue-collar worker's real income is rising at some 3 percent per year, then he will perhaps believe that there is enough here for all

---
* Governor of Alabama George Wallace.

of us chickens and accept the integration of Negros into the labor force and efforts to improve the relative lot of the Negro. However, halt his progress and the resistance to income distribution efforts will increase.

But to return to the major theme: if income distribution is the name of the game, and if the distribution of income is to be "rectified" by biasing the distribution of growth, then it is necessary for the overall growth rate to be sufficiently high so that a substantial growth in income for all except perhaps the very top can be sustained. If Baumol's disease is in one of its more virulent phases—due perhaps to bureaucratic and institutional as well as to technological reasons—then the potential for biasing growth in disposable income is diminished. Under these circumstances we could expect more virulent opposition to income redistribution as well as more persistent demands for change.

Note also that the bureaucratic resistance to change may be reinforced by slow growth. If the prospects for improvement are not all that great there will be an intensified effort to protect what one has. Britain may be a prize example of this phenomenon.

[. . .]*

The Stability, Perhaps Perversity, of Relative Wages

The distribution of income from work depends upon relative wages. In the original poverty numbers a large percentage of those in poverty worked full time during the year. If the distribution of relative wages can be affected by policy or by the behavior of the economy, then the possibility exists that poverty can be eased by relative wage changes.

Note that income from work is only a part of total income; that the overall income distribution includes income from property (interest and profits) and capital gains in excess of price level increases. During the period under consideration, the 1960s to date, there was a run-up of corporate profits after taxes and sizable capital gains resulted from the run of success the economy experienced.[3]

---

* An Appendix, located here in the manuscript, has been moved to the end of the current chapter.

Figure 3.1

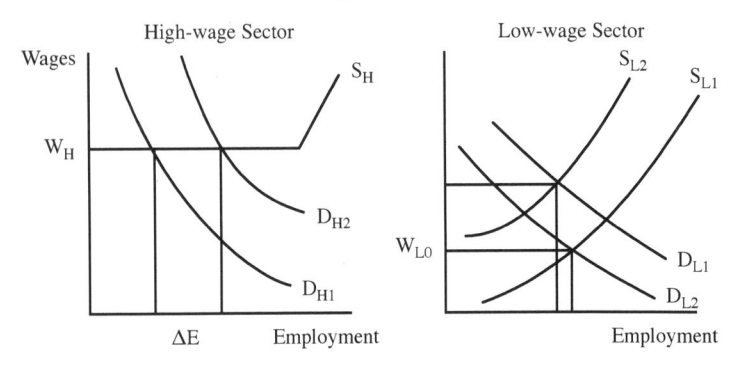

These factors tended to bias the distribution of the increments of income toward the wealthier. However, the distribution of income from property, or even the share of income going to property, is not of special interest to the poor and not-well-off portions of the population: their income is derived from work, and for their income to gain on the average income it must first improve relative to other incomes from work.

A simple model of "high" wage and "low" wage industries, in which, in order to be selective, high-wage industries attempt to keep their wages at a premium over other wages during a period of normal slack in the labor market, indicates that in a period of tightening labor markets, low wages will tend to rise more rapidly than high wages. The high-wage sector sets a money wage W_H, so that its supply of labor is infinitely elastic at this wage.

A rise in demand increases employment, at an unchanged money wage. The supply schedule of labor to the low-wage sector is some market supply curve minus employment in the high-wage sector. A rise in employment in the high-wage sector shifts the supply curve of the low-wage sector to the left: S_{L1} shifts to S_{L2}. The rise in overall demand that shifted the demand curve for labor in the high-wage sector up also shifts the demand curve for labor in the low-wage sector to the right. Thus wages in the low-wage sector rise from W_{L0} to W_{L1}, and given an invariant wage in the high-wage sector W_H, the ratio of low to high wages rises.

Policy and Poverty (1969)

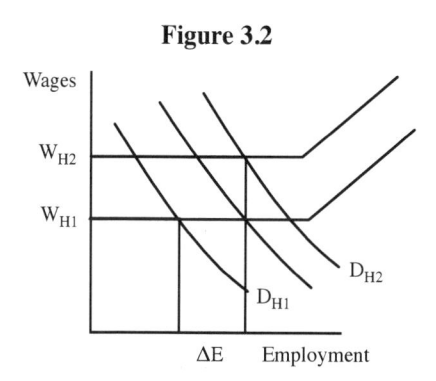

Figure 3.2

[Figure 3.2: Graph with Wages on vertical axis showing W_{H2} above W_{H1}, and Employment on horizontal axis with ΔE marked. Demand curves D_{H1} and D_{H2} shown.]

An alternative model, using the same format, would have W_H as some ratio to low wages. If the high wages are in "administered" industries, then the price of the product could be set as some mark up on wages. In this case, a rise in W_H will also shift D_H up by the same amount. Thus, in Figure 3.2, the rise to W_{H2} and D_{H2} means that the change in employment ΔE remains the same, but the relative wages of high- and low-wage workers has remained unchanged.

If the model of Figure 3.1 is relevant, then a protracted period of full employment, and in particular, a period of relatively tight full employment such as we have witnessed since 1965, should result in a narrowing of the spread among wages. It also means that sustaining full employment would be a weapon for the elimination of poverty above and beyond its impact on the unemployed and the underemployed. If the model of Figure 3.2 is relevant, then no improvement in the status of the low-wage worker can be expected from high employment aside from that due to the rise in employment.

In the 10 years 1959 through 1968, the total number of persons in poverty fell from 38.9 million to 22 million. In the eight years from 1960 through 1967, the percentage of white families living in poverty fell from 18.1 percent to 10.2 percent; the percentage of nonwhite families living in poverty fell from 55.1 percent to 35.3 percent. Even though some of the credit may go to various training and community action programs, the decline in poverty seems most closely related to the rise in employment, including the increase in the armed forces.

Table 3.3 Employment and Armed Forces (in thousands), Unemployment Rate, and the Incidence of Poverty, 1958–68

Year	Employment*	Change in Employment	Armed Forces*	Change in Armed Forces	Change in Forces and Employment	Unemployment Rate*	Total #	Total %	White #	White %	Nonwhite #	Nonwhite %
1958	63,036	—	2,636	—	—	6.8	—	—	—	—	—	—
1959	64,630	1,594	2,552	-84	1,510	5.5	38.9	22.1	28.2	18.0	10.7	54.6
1960	65,778	1,148	2,514	-38	1,110	5.5	40.1	22.3	28.7	18.1	11.4	55.1
1961	65,746	-38	2,572	58	20	6.7	38.1	21.0	26.5	16.5	11.6	55.4
1962	66,702	956	2,828	256	1,212	5.5	37.0	20.1	25.4	15.6	11.6	54.2
1963	67,762	1,060	2,738	-90	970	5.7	35.3	18.9	24.1	14.6	11.2	50.9
1964	69,305	1,543	2,739	1	1,544	5.2	34.3	18.1	23.4	14.0	10.8	48.6
1965	71,088	1,783	2,723	-16	1,767	4.5	31.9	16.7	21.4	12.7	10.5	46.4
1966	72,895	1,807	3,123	400	2,207	3.8	28.8	14.9	19.5	11.5	9.3	40.0
1967	74,372	1,477	3,446	323	1,800	3.8	25.9	13.3	17.6	10.2	8.3	35.3
1968	75,920	1,548	3,535	89	1,637	3.6	22.0	—	—	—	—	—

Incidence of Poverty Persons in Families and Unrelated Individuals in Poverty (in millions)

Sources: *CEA (1969), Table B-22, 252; **Census Bureau (1968), Table 2: Incidence of Poverty

Policy and Poverty (1969)

The impact of tight labor markets upon the population in poverty seems clearest when attention is focused upon the nonwhites in poverty. In 1960 some 55.1 percent, in 1963 some 50.9 percent, in 1966 some 40 percent and in 1967 some 35.3 percent of nonwhite families were living in poverty. In 1960 the overall unemployment rate was 5.5 percent, in 1963 the unemployment rate was 5.7 percent, [and] in 1966 and 1967 the unemployment rate was 3.8 percent. Between 1960 and 1967, the armed services increased by more than 900,000 and "civilian" employment by more than eight million. It seems evident that the benefits to the nonwhite from the sustained prosperity lagged behind the benefits to the whites.

It was only after the overall unemployment rate was lowered from the neighborhood of 5.5 percent to the neighborhood of 4 percent that an appreciable dent was made in the proportion of nonwhites in poverty.

From the evidence in Table 3.3 it seems clear that the rise in employment (including the rise in the armed forces) can be used to explain the decline in the population in poverty. The war on poverty has in effect followed an employment strategy—although the initial gains in employment were not distributed so as to achieve a maximum impact upon the population in poverty. The employment strategy actually followed was not efficient either in terms of the initial impacted population or the bundle of goods produced with respect to the goal of ending poverty. The power of adequate employment opportunities is perhaps made clear by the success in decreasing poverty of even the poorly designed employment program that in fact was implemented. We can only conjecture at the impact that a high-employment policy especially designed to reduce poverty would have upon the population in poverty.

Tighter full employment can help the poor in three ways: by moving a family from unemployed to employed status, by eliminating short-time and partial unemployment, and by raising relative wages. The available evidence indicates that there has been no improvement in the distribution of income from work, relative wages have not improved over the long expansion of the 1960s, and over

Table 3.4 Ratio of Average Weekly Earnings to Average Weekly Earnings in All Manufacturing, 1948, 1953, 1960, 1966, 1967

Industry	1948	1953	1960	1966	1967
Mining	1.234	1.178	1.175	1.158	1.186
Contract Construction	1.228	1.226	1.259	1.293	1.338
Ordnance and Accessories	1.078	1.108	1.208	1.209	1.182
Lumber and Wood Products	0.896	0.862	0.821	0.825	0.837
Furniture and Fixtures	0.919	0.893	0.838	0.813	0.816
Stone, Clay, and Glass Products	1.001	0.995	1.031	1.018	1.025
Primary Metal Industries	1.151	1.198	1.221	1.230	1.192
Fabricated Metal Products	1.060	1.085	1.096	1.084	1.073
Machinery	1.136	1.173	1.165	1.202	1.183
Electrical Equipment	1.026	1.000	1.011	0.969	0.969
Transportation Equipment	1.162	1.210	1.242	1.267	1.233
Instruments and Related Products	0.989	1.030	1.040	1.010	1.018
Miscellaneous Manufacturing	0.904	0.873	0.827	0.791	0.802
Food and Kindred Products	0.920	0.901	0.959	0.925	0.940
Tobacco Manufactures	0.689	0.675	0.723	0.758	0.762
Textile Mill Products	0.822	0.754	0.708	0.731	0.733
Apparel and Related Products	0.822	0.691	0.627	0.613	0.636
Paper and Allied Products	1.030	1.019	1.060	1.063	1.069
Printing and Publishing	1.226	1.167	1.147	1.092	1.096
Chemicals and Allied Products	1.041	1.053	1.150	1.118	1.122
Petroleum and Related Products	1.304	1.282	1.322	1.288	1.330
Rubber and Plastic Products	1.004	1.031	1.031	0.995	0.987
Leather and Leather Products	0.773	0.722	0.674	0.667	0.687
Wholesale Trade	1.009	0.978	1.011	0.990	1.013
Retail Trade	0.784	0.705	0.695	0.611	0.617

Source: Computed from Department of Labor (1968), Table C-6: Gross Average Weekly Earnings of Production or Non-Supervisory Workers on Payrolls of Selected Industries Annual Averages

Policy and Poverty (1969)

Table 3.5 Distribution of Relative Wages (all manufacturing = 100): Average Weekly Earnings in 21 Manufacturing Industries, Mining, Construction, and Trade, 1948, 1953, 1960, 1966, 1967

Weekly Wage as a Percentage of Wage in All Manufacturing	Number of Industries				
	1948	1953	1960	1966	1967
125.0+	1	1	2	3	2
115.0–124.9	5	6	6	5	5
105.0–114.9	3	3	3	3	4
95.0–104.9	7	6	6	5	5
85.0–94.9	4	4	—	1	1
75.0–84.9	4	1	3	4	4
65.0–74.9	1	4	4	2	2
64.9 or less	—	—	1	2	2

Source: Table 3.4

the longer run (since the end of World War II) the evidence indicates that a deterioration in relative wages has occurred.

Table 3.4 shows the distribution of relative weekly wages in various manufacturing industries, mining, construction, and trade. The data are summarized in Table 3.5.

At the end of World War II, the distribution of weekly wages was closely bunched around the average for all manufacturing. Some seven industries fell into the 95–104.9 percent of all manufacturing range; some 14 industries fell in the range of 85–114.9 percent of all manufacturing. In 1948, for only one industry was the average income more than 125 percent of the all manufacturing range; for only one industry was the weekly wage less than 75 percent of the average weekly wage.

In the postwar period a thinning out of the midrange of weekly wages occurred. In 1960, only six industries were in the 95 percent to 104.9 percent range and only three more were in the 105–114.9 percent range; the 85–94.9 percent range was empty. In the period since 1960 a further widening of the range has occurred, so that in 1967 only five industries remain in the 95–104.9 percent range, two

Table 3.6 Coefficients of Variation of Hourly and Weekly Earnings, 1960–67

	Hourly Earnings			Weekly Earnings		
Year	Total	Excluding Finance	Excluding Finance and Trade	Total	Excluding Finance	Excluding Finance and Trade
1960	23.42	24.12	18.69	25.78	26.52	19.86
1961	23.22	24.05	18.45	26.33	27.15	20.07
1962	22.66	23.33	18.57	25.81	26.61	19.38
1963	21.89	22.82	17.99	25.82	26.68	19.28
1964	22.10	22.85	18.55	26.39	27.08	20.17
1965	22.68	23.49	19.45	27.32	28.13	20.68
1966	21.58	22.39	18.29	27.67	28.48	20.09
1967	21.75	22.52	18.52	27.76	28.55	20.45

industries are in excess of 130 percent of all manufacturing, and two are less than 65 percent of all manufacturing. In 1948 the lowest wage (tobacco manufacturing) was 68.9 percent of the average and the highest wage (petroleum and related products) was 130.4 percent of all manufacturing. In 1967 retail trade was 61.7 percent, apparel and related trades was 63.6 percent, while contract construction was 133.8 percent and petroleum and related products was 133 percent of the average of all manufacturing.

Thus it seems as if the post–World War II period has seen a dispersion of relative wages and the tighter labor markets of the late 1960s did not lead to a narrowing of the range. Of course, in 1968 labor markets were even tighter than in 1967, and perhaps a narrowing of the range did occur. However, the hope that a little more will make a big difference seems like a weak reed for an economic policy to lean on.

The coefficient of variation is the standard deviation divided by the arithmetic mean. It is a "deunitized" measure of dispersion. Over the extended expansion of the 1960s the coefficient of variation of hourly earnings exhibited some decrease, whereas the coefficient of variation of weekly earnings showed some increase. This means that whereas relative hourly wages tended to draw together, overtime and layoffs tended to widen the distribution of income. Over this period of sustained prosperity and tightening full employment, the behavior of hourly rates conformed to the model in which extended prosperity narrows the range of wages but the changes in hours worked offset this tendency so that the range of weekly earnings widened.

It is worth noting that the distribution of hourly earnings is not as dispersed as that of weekly earnings, that the dispersion is relatively narrow when finance and trade are excluded, and that for both hourly and weekly earnings — but especially for hourly earnings — the coefficient of variation excluding finance and trade did not exhibit much of a trend. Thus we can infer that in the relatively more highly unionized manufacturing, mining, and construction sectors the dispersion of wages did not change much over the decade. In addition, the differential between hourly wages in trade and finance and in manufacturing narrowed over the decade while the differential in weekly wages widened.

The evidence from the coefficients of variation is consistent with the evidence from the analysis of the behavior of relative wages by industry. The period of the 1960s did not see any narrowing of the spread of wages. If such a narrowing had taken place the income of the low-wage retail trade and apparel workers would have been substantially higher. For example, if these workers received 80 percent rather than 62 percent or 64 percent of all the manufacturing average, their income would have been about 30 percent higher and the number of families [in close proximity] to poverty would have been appreciably reduced (some 10 million workers are in the four sectors in which income is less than 75 percent of the average in all manufacturing) compared to the actual 1967 situation.

Thus the labor markets as they behaved during the 1960s did not tend to reduce the inequality of incomes as unemployment rates were lowered and kept low. Thus one possible benefit from a full employment policy did not appear. Relative wages were either sticky or perverse. The question is open whether some alternative form of labor market behavior and organization would lead to a different pattern of relative wage and income changes during periods of economic expansion. As things stand, we must plan policy on the assumption that the pattern of relative wages is stable, and that if the pattern is to be changed, some institutional changes will be needed.

The Feedbacks from Sustained Tight Full Employment

The general success of Keynesian economic policy during the eight Kennedy–Johnson years is not to be doubted, even though the [period 1965–68], which is perhaps of greatest interest, might be classified as a "classical" war rather than a "Keynesian" innovative period in economic policy. The validity of an employment strategy as the rock upon which a serious antipoverty war is to be based is clear from the experience of the past four years. In effect, during these years a poorly designed employment policy was associated with a sharp decrease in the population in poverty.

Policy and Poverty (1969)

The employment policy was poorly designed from the point of view of a campaign to eliminate poverty. It was not directed at the poor, but rather at a perceived generalized deficiency in aggregate demand. During this period, the available socially and politically approved spending was heavily biased toward military spending (the war in Vietnam was helpful), which in an age of research directly benefits the well-to-do. Furthermore, the tax relief granted during this period in order to sustain demand benefited property owners and other high incomes. The employment strategy was implemented by trickle-down tactics.

Nevertheless, even though the target of spending was not the poor, the very fact that tight labor markets were attained and sustained for many months has resulted in an improvement in the lot of the poor. If tight labor markets were continued, a further increase in the proportion of the population in the pool of experienced workers could be expected to take place. Sustaining tight full employment is necessary to hold the gains that have been made, as well as to make further gains possible. Are there any fundamental and strong forces in a capitalist economy which tend to make the sustaining of full employment politically unpopular, unproductive in reducing poverty, or very difficult?

The answer to the question is that there are. "Inflation," especially if it is accelerating, decreases the political popularity of full employment. A rise in the relative wages of urban civic employees (teachers, policemen, firemen, etc.) may, given the limited fiscal power of urban governments, lead to a deterioration of the income provided through public goods. In addition, the upward instability of investment demand combined with the financial repercussions of an investment boom may make it very difficult to sustain full employment.

Inflation

Milton Friedman and some of his disciples have taken to characterizing the decrease in unemployment rates in the recent past as "inflation induced" decreases in unemployment. This terminology runs counter to the Phillips curve language, popular in this country

following a terrific performance put on by Samuelson and Solow*
at the annual meetings of the economists in December 1960, which
associates the rate of change in money wages with the unemployment rate (Samuelson and Solow 1960). The rate of change in money
prices is less than the rate of change in money wages because of productivity increases. Thus, in the Samuelson-Solow-Phillips model, a
tightening of labor markets is associated with rising prices and wages,
but as wages rise faster than prices, the real wage increases. In this
world the previously employed and the newly employed both benefit—in fact, as the differential between the rate at which wages and
prices change is often assumed to be an invariant, reflecting productivity changes, the improvement of the continuously employed worker's lot is independent of the unemployment rate. Thus, as it costs the
previously employed workers nothing, they might as well accept the
decrease in unemployment. It is a world of "social harmony."

The Friedman world is not a world of social harmony—class
conflicts can rage. An excess of aggregate demand over aggregate
supply (the excessive aggregate demand is due to too large a rate of
growth in the money supply) raises prices relative to wages. This
lowers the real wage of workers and as a result employment increases. The rise in prices in excess of the rise in wages lowers the real
income of the previously employed workers, making them worse
off; the workers moving from being unemployed to being employed
are better off. Thus, in the Friedmanite world, the profit taker, who
gains from rising prices, and the poor benefit from tight labor markets, the regularly employed worker loses.

It seems as if the Friedmanite picture had some validity in 1968.
The previous year or so had seen industrial workers' wage rates lag a
bit behind price increases. Thus resentment at the state of the world,
which was improving the lot of the others at the expense of the
steadily employed, existed and perhaps found a political expression
in [pro-Wallace] sentiment.

Thus the [view that] wage rate increases associated with low
unemployment generate inflation . . . looks upon inflation as socially benign; the inflation-induced view of how low unemployment

---
* Paul Samuelson and Robert Solow.

rates are achieved sees inflation as socially corrosive. If benign, low unemployment rates plus inflation can continue indefinitely and need not accelerate; if corrosive, then low unemployment rates cannot continue indefinitely, especially in a nonhomogeneous society, and as the losers, or nongainers, try to maintain or improve their position it might very well accelerate.

Sustained low unemployment rates are an exotic environment; American capitalism hasn't been in this climate for at least 40 years, if ever. The question of whether a given rate of inflation will be associated with a given unemployment rate depends in the Friedmanite view upon whether the productivity of the workers whose employment is induced by inflation is permanently increased. If so, then high employment will no longer depend upon a lowering of real wages through inflation. The "natural" or "noninflationary" employment level is increased.

In the Phillips view a similar leavening process would shift the relation between price level increases and employment, so that each unemployment rate is associated with a smaller rise in prices.

If the need for inflation to induce lower unemployment is transitory, then in time the inflation-induced decline in income of the prior employed will come to a halt. The period of social conflict between the newly and the steadily employed will be relatively short and perhaps we can afford it. If no such shift occurred, then socially the aggregate demand technique for ending poverty via employment is a blocked path.

The Wages of Public Employees

Income includes the services received in kind from the public sector. Most of these services, especially the traditional education, health, recreation, and public protection, can be considered to be labor intensive. As was shown earlier, these sections may be both nonprogressive and blessed with an income elastic demand. Thus, as time goes on, the labor supply and the relative burden associated with these sectors may increase. However, there is another important element, quite independent of the progress and demand factors, that will make the costs of public sector output rise relative to the cost of private goods.

The expectation that full employment will be sustained affects the relative attractiveness of different occupations. Highly seasonal and cyclical industries and occupations need to pay a premium in hourly or weekly wages over occupations which are not affected by such fluctuations. This is necessary in order to compensate the workers for the uncertainty they carry.

The expected utility to workers from different occupations for those free to choose among occupations will be equal. But to risk averters the expected utility associated with a fluctuating income is less than the expected utility associated with a stable income with the same expected value. That is, making $100 a week half the time and $200 a week the other half of the time yields a smaller expected utility than earning $150 a week all the time.

The simple expected utility calculus needs to be modified depending upon whether fluctuations in income are associated with leisure as a good and whether fluctuating amounts of leisure per week are preferred or are inferior to an equal average but stable amount of leisure per week. However, the main modification that has to be made is whether the fluctuating pattern is known with certainty (fully anticipated) or conjectural.

We can assume that seasonal patterns of employment are known with [near] certainty and that cyclical patterns are conjectural. Thus, if there were only seasonal (fully anticipated) fluctuations in employment, the average income over a set of seasons of like labor in different occupations would tend to equalize. However, occupations with unanticipated fluctuations in employment, fluctuations that cannot be forecast with certainty, will need to pay a premium income in order to attract a given class of labor: the expected income in the occupations with cyclically fluctuating incomes will need to be greater than the expected income from cyclically stable occupations.

Public service employment is insulated from all but truly major business declines. The hours, wages, and incomes enjoy large protections against cyclical declines in income. Thus, in a world in which cyclical fluctuations in income are important, public employees can be expected to earn less on the average than employees in the cyclically sensitive private sector.

If due to a change in the performance of the economy the expectation that cyclical fluctuations are expected to occur is diminished, then the premium of cyclical over stable incomes will need to decrease. However, such an attenuation of the expectations that business depressions will occur takes place only after an extended run of prosperous times. Thus it will be associated with full employment and sectoral excess demand for labor. The adjustment of the two classes of wages to the change in expectations will take place by a rapid increase of public sector wages in order to catch up with private sector wages. There will be an independent impact from full employment expectations tending to make the public sector's costs rise relative to those in the private sector.

As a result of this phenomenon, a deterioration of the public sector or a sharp rise in costs may be expected to occur after an extended period of full employment. To the extent that the antipoverty strategy is based upon full employment plus a rise in public goods production, the rise in relative wages of public sector employees as a result of full employment is a barrier that might frustrate the policy goal. However, this barrier depends upon the political and social reaction to higher taxes—and will in part depend upon whether the gains from full employment and the income from improvements in public goods are so shared as to be conducive to an acceptance of higher relative costs.

The Financial Barrier to Sustaining Full Employment

The 1960s to date have been a most successful period, if success is measured by the absence of a recession, the growth in real GNP, and the reduction in the percentage of the population measured as living in poverty. Aside from the accelerated rise in price level since 1964 (which was coincident with the reduction in the unemployment rate and the proportion of nonwhites in poverty), the major flaw of the 1960s is that wants expanded at least as fast as output—especially wants for wars and other public goods—so that a feeling of general impoverishment has accompanied the great enrichment. Obviously, the problem of scarcity remains as long as wants are expandable; true affluence will follow upon a restriction of wants.

However, even though wants expand as fast as or faster than capacity, it nevertheless is true that much of the observed decline in poverty is the result of the expansion being sustained since 1961. The population in poverty would increase sharply if unemployment rates ever jumped to, say, 6.8 percent or 8.8 percent from the 3.6 percent of 1968. Continued success in reducing poverty depends critically upon sustaining full employment and even making labor markets tighter than they have been to date.

However, it may very well be that sustaining an expansion is inherently impossible in an economy such as the United States. The United States is an intensely financial and basically a highly competitive capitalist economy. The very productivity and responsiveness of output to consumer preferences is due to the way in which investment responds to profit opportunities and the way in which financing for such investment is made available through a flexible financial system. Thus the essential characteristic of American capitalism is a widespread willingness and ability to engage in speculation.

In a world where the memory of past recessions and depressions persists, a run of very good years will tend to attenuate if not erase such memories. But these memories find their expression in liability structures of firms and preferred asset holdings of both households and financial institutions. An attenuation or erasure of such memories will lead to sharp changes in portfolio preference. These changes have two results: an investment boom and a sharp rise in interest rates as demand for investment and position-taking financing increases. The rise in interest rates causes both losses to owners of previously issued long-term debt securities, and a higher ratio of cash payment commitments to expected cash receipts by those financing either investment or positions in inherited assets.

The investment boom together with its financial repercussions will initially lead to an accelerating expansion that carries demand beyond full employment demand—which means price level increases. Either because of endogenous limits to how much financing can be extracted from a given financial system or policy actions designed to dampen an inflationary expansion, a break in the explosive expansion will take place. This can lead to a sharp decline in asset values and, following a "liquidity crisis," a sharp reduction in investment demand. A rather serious recession or depression can follow.[4]

In 1966 such a process occurred, leading to a mini-panic (called "the crunch") around Labor Day of that year. The serious recession or depression did not occur because fiscal policy stepped in [almost] immediately with a sharp rise in Vietnam War expenditures. The rise in military expenditures in 1966–67 really is a well-nigh perfect example of how government expenditures should rise to prevent a near crash in the financial sector from accelerating to a full-blown panic, and to abort a sharp decline in income and employment.

It is also evident from the events of 1966–67 that a well-nigh perfect use of coordinated monetary and fiscal policy can prevent the quite awful consequences of a sharp fall in income from occurring, but only at a price that includes a quite quick recovery of the inflationary pressures. To constrain the explosive tendencies of American capitalism it might very well be true that a more serious set of financial losses and declines in production than occurred in 1966–67 may be needed. This would carry with it a rise in poverty via a rise in unemployment.

Thus it may be true that the explosive forces in American capitalism make it impossible to sustain extended periods of full employment, such as we have enjoyed in the 1960s. Thus the path to universal affluence through perpetual prosperity may be blocked.

Conclusion

By any reasonable view of how fast is fast, the years since 1964 have seen a sharp reduction of the population in measured poverty. This success has been mainly due to the rise in employment—including the armed forces—and little or none of it can be imputed to an improvement in the relative incomes of the low-paid employed worker. That is, poverty has been reduced because of a change from unemployment, not because the relative income of those in poverty, even though fully employed during the year, has risen. The industrial wage structure has not changed in the desired way.

It also seems evident that there are sharp limitations on what can be done by transfer payments. In particular, the labor force participation and the savings reaction together with the GNP and economic growth targets make it likely that any broad improvement in the transfer payments schemes will be inflated out. Thus, if transfer payment schemes are introduced, they should be accompanied with incentives for labor market participation by revising Social Security, lowering the school-leaving age, [establishing] preferential tax treatment of apprentice income and costs, etc. Ever since the Keynesian revolution, those facets of the welfare system that were, in effect, introduced to lower labor market participation have been obsolete.

It also seems true that a highly urbanized environment, carrying with it a demand for labor-intensive services, may be growth retarding. Thus the possibilities of alleviating poverty or generating equality by biasing the distribution of increments to income may be limited by a slowdown in the rate of growth of income.

If we add to this urbanization phenomenon the impact of the attenuation of uncertainty upon relative wages it seems clear that the cost per unit of publicly supplied "goods and services" as well as the relative quantity of such goods and services in GNP will rise with both economic growth and economic success. The shift in the proportions of public to private output will obviously have an impact upon the willingness of taxpayers to support programs which yield them no obvious or perceived benefits.

It also seems evident that sustained full employment may not affect relative wages in such a manner as to raise low wages relative to high wages: the terms of trade do not seem to move in favor of the low-wage earner during sustained prosperity.

The marked decrease in the numbers living in poverty during the 1960s was mainly due to a run of prosperous years. The financial disruption of 1966 and the even tighter financial market conditions of recent months indicate that it may be impossible to sustain tight full employment and economic growth. If this is so, then the goal of eliminating poverty or equalizing income is even more difficult to attain within our institutional structure than the success of the past few years would indicate.

A gimmick or a good idea is not sufficient for successful economic policy. Meaningful economic policy must be consistent with the underlying behavioral rules of the economy. One behavioral rule is that a willingness to pay taxes and support programs that involve taxes depends upon the benefits the taxpayer perceives. A welfare program yields little—once true starvation and public begging are eliminated—to all but the most altruistic of taxpayers. Parks, public safety, clean streets, and even the education of others yield perceptible or available benefits to [nearly] all taxpayers. The ability to achieve a radical—or even a modest—income equalization through public expenditures depends upon the public program yielding perceived benefits to those who sacrifice in the form of taxes for the project. If a growth in the public sector can be achieved which yields the equivalent of a 0.5 percent per year increase in private income to the representative taxpayer (as well as a somewhat larger income equivalent to lower income households), then it is possible that radical income equalization would be acceptable. That is, a work program that yields rapidly rising money income to the additional public employees while it yields perceptible and recognized benefits to others than those employed in the program is a feasible way of equalizing income.

Whether it takes the form of wage subsidies to privately employed workers or government direct demand for labor and supply of particular outputs is not relevant. What is most relevant is that any program of income equalization yield benefits—such as postal services, or even cheap food—to those who pay the taxes. Expensive income equalization programs cannot depend upon altruism—public goods may provide the vehicle by which self-interest is consistent with income equalization. Thus, no income equalization program is truly feasible unless it provides for an increase of labor force participation and in output.

Suggestions have been made that the government be the employer of last resort. In any such program the government would presumably set a wage rate at which it is willing to employ all available workers. This wage rate immediately becomes a wage floor for all sectors, hence I labeled an employer-of-last-resort program as a wage support law; the terms upon which the government stands ready to employ all is analogous to the farm price support programs.

If we look upon wage support as a technique for generating services from the public sector, then there will be benefits to all from the program. If it is possible to constrain the highest-wage industries while allowing the wage support level to rise faster than prices, then a wage support law might be able to narrow the range of wages. One of the very high-wage industries is contract construction. The government is a major purchaser of the output of contract construction. The government might be able to set a ceiling on how rapidly it will allow such wages to increase. Such a program of restraint in high wages will need to be accompanied by equitable and biting taxation of property and other high incomes.

The urban plight calls for an enlarged public and urban service sector. The needs of wage equalization call for expanded government employment at improving wages. Such programs could yield visible benefits to the nonpoor, thus it may be feasible.

Poverty in America will not be eliminated by simple programs which naively assume that all is possible. There is a serious doubt that a program can be devised to overcome or circumvent what are the more obvious barriers to success in such an effort. However, without awareness of the barriers it truly would be a fluke if a successful program were devised.

Appendix: An Arithmetic Example of Baumol's Disease

Assume that final demand is such that the "physical" output of the two sectors is equal at all times. Thus workers will be shifted from the technologically progressive sector to the technologically stagnant sectors. Assume that wages are set in the progressive sector and that wages determine prices so that the nominal price per unit of the output of the progressive sector remains constant. Wages are the same in the two sectors, thus the price per unit of output in the

Policy and Poverty (1969)

stagnant sector rises at the same rate as productivity increases. It is clear that as this process continues, the labor force will be switched from the progressive to the stagnant sector, the growth rate of output will decrease, and the rate of increase in the price level will asymptotically approach the rate of increase in productivity.

Let us assume that initially we have 200 workers, 100 assigned to each sector. Wages equal $1 per period in both sectors; the value of output is $200 per period. Output per man hour grows at 6 percent per period in the progressive sector. In order to keep output the same in the two sectors, some three workers are shifted from the progressive to the stationary sector for the second period. Wages now equal $1.06, output in each sector is 1.03, the total value of output is $212.18, the growth rate of output is 3 percent, and the price index has risen from 100 to 103.

If 150 workers are assigned to the stagnant sector and 50 to the progressive sector, then the output per man in the progressive sector will need to be three times the output of the first example. In this case, wages will be $3 per period and total output is 300 units. The value of output in the stagnant sector is $450 [and] in the progressive sector it is $150, so that GNP is 600. The price level is 2.0. Labor productivity in the progressive sector grows at a 6 percent rate, so that at the end of one period productivity in the progressive sector is 3.18. As a result, 2.15 workers will need to be shifted to the stagnant sector, the wage rate will rise to $3.18, and the value of output in the progressive sector is $152.15 and in the stagnant sector it becomes $483.85. Real output has grown from 300 to 304.3, or approximately 1.5 percent. The money value of income produced rises to $636 so that the GNP deflator rises from 2.0 to 2.09, i.e., by 4.5 percent.

In the third case the initial conditions are 10 workers in the progressive sector and 190 in the stagnant sector. The productivity in the progressive sector is now 19 times as great as in the stagnant sector so that output is 190 in each sector; real GNP is 380. Market value of GNP is $3,800, so the price level is 10.0. After one period, some 0.54 workers need to be shifted to the stagnant sector to maintain equality of output in the two sectors. The real value of GNP rises to 381.08; real growth is some 0.3 of 1 percent. The wage rate rises to 20.14; market value of output is 4,028. The price level is 10.57; a 5.7 percent increase in prices has taken place.

Notes

1. If real GNP grows at 4.5 percent and population at 1 percent, then per capita income would grow at 3.5 percent. As the amount needed for redistribution will decrease due to the smaller population and as the growth in total GNP has increased, the amount available in each year to make the well-off better off increases.
2. An alternative growth model posits that there are two sectors—a high- and a low-productivity sector. Both of these sectors are stagnant; productivity in each sector remains constant but output grows as a result of labor shifting from the low- to the high-productivity sector. Obviously, in such a world, in time, growth ceases once all labor is in the high-productivity sector.
3. The argument that a rise in investment relative to income leads to a rise in the ratio of profits to income is closely identified with Kaldor (1956).
4. The model in which full employment growth cannot be sustained because of financial factors is stated in greater detail in Minsky (1969). (See also Minsky 1968a; 1968b.)

Sources

Baumol, W. J. 1967. "Macroeconomics of Unbalanced Growth: The Anatomy of Urban Crisis." *The American Economic Review* 57(3): 414–26.

CEA (Council of Economic Advisers). 1969. *Economic Report of the President*. Washington, D.C.: Government Printing Office. January.

Census Bureau. 1968. *Current Population Reports: Consumer Income*. Series P-60, No. 55. Washington, D.C.: Government Printing Office. August.

Department of Labor. 1968. *Manpower Report of the President*. Washington, D.C.: Government Printing Office.

Kaldor, N. 1955–56. "Alternative Theories of Distribution." *The Review of Economic Studies* 23(2): 83–100.

Minsky, H. P. 1968a. "The Crunch and Its Aftermath." 1968. *Bankers Magazine* 205 (February): 78–82 and (March): 171–73.

———. 1968b. "The Crunch of 1966—Model for New Financial Crises?" *Transaction* 5(4): 44–51.

———. 1969. "Private Sector Asset Management and the Effectiveness of Monetary Policy: Theory and Practice." *Journal of Finance* 24(2): 223–38.

Samuelson, P. A., and R. N. Solow. 1960. "Analytical Aspects of Anti-Inflation Policy." *The American Economic Review* 50(2): 177–94.

Scitovsky, T. 1964. "Equity." In *Papers on Welfare and Growth*. Palo Alto, Calif.: Stanford University Press.

Chapter 4

The Macroeconomics of a Negative Income Tax*
(1969)

Introduction

From time to time public policy proposals which once were far out quite suddenly achieve social respectability. This seems to be the case with the "social dividend" when it is dressed up in its currently more fashionable garb as a "negative income tax." A social dividend is very simple. It transfers to every person alive, rich or poor, working or unemployed, young or old, a designated money income by right. Income taxes are paid on receipts from work, property, or other transfer schemes. Such taxable income is defined in the tax code, and, almost without exception, in the various tax codes income in the form of the services of owned property or "household" labor is not included in tax code income. Thus private disposable income is the social dividend plus tax code income minus taxes.

A negative income tax is rather more sophisticated in form. It transfers to every eligible unit a cash payment which is some portion of the difference between its actual and some designated, or target, tax code income.

For example, for a household of four the social dividend might be worth $3,000 per year and a tax of one-third might be levied on "tax code" income. Thus no tax code income results in $3,000 of disposable income, $6,000 of tax code income results in $7,000 of disposable income, ($3,000 + two-thirds of $6,000), $9,000 of tax code income results in $9,000 of disposable income, and $12,000 of tax code income results in $11,000 of disposable income.

A negative income tax is designed to supplement private income from work, property, or transfers by making up a portion of the difference between tax code income and a target income. Thus a scheme equivalent to the above social dividend would add to private disposable income one-third of the difference between such income

---

* Paper 429, Hyman P. Minsky Archive, Levy Economics Institute, Annandale-on-Hudson, N.Y. The original draft of this paper was read at the Conference on Income and Poverty, sponsored by the American Academy of Arts and Sciences and held at Washington University–St. Louis, May 16–17, 1969.

and $9,000. Once again, zero tax code income results in $3,000 of disposable income, $6,000 results in $7,000 of disposable income, $9,000 results in $9,000, and $12,000 will pay a net tax of one-third on ($12,000 − $9,000), resulting in $11,000 of disposable income.

There are three "parameters" to a social dividend or negative income tax: the minimum guarantee, the tax rate on earned income, and the break-even or target income where disposable income equals earned income. Once any two of the parameters are given, the third can be computed. A negative income tax scheme fixes the target income ($9,000 in our example) and the tax rate. The minimum income is computed. A social dividend fixes the minimum income ($3,000 in our example) and the tax rate. The break-even or target income is computed.[1]

Thus the two schemes are identical in substance; only the label is different. Administratively, a social dividend seems simpler, and I venture to guess that if adopted the form will be that of a social dividend and the language that of a negative income tax. In terms of the analysis that follows, the impacts of a negative income tax on the various relations might be seen more clearly if it is assumed that each family receives a monthly check which is determined solely by family size: for the family of four in the examples above the monthly check will be $250.

There are great differences among the various proposals, however labeled. These differences relate to the scale or generosity of the proposal.[2] Perhaps the general idea is popular because the various proposals so differ in scale, cost, and objective that it is possible to be for the idea for many different reasons. Some proposals are not offered as a solution to poverty, defined in terms of the adequacy of private disposable income; they are offered as solutions to the social and administrative messes that are presumed to characterize existing welfare and income-supplement schemes.[3]

Proposals which distribute no more to the present poor than the existing programs but which do it more efficiently and humanely are not at issue. Reforms of welfare for such objectives might very well be a "no-loss" game: there are savings and benefits without any appreciable costs or losses.

The Macroeconomics of a Negative Income Tax (1969)

What is at issue is the efficacy of a negative income tax as an instrument in an effort to eliminate poverty, defined in terms of some absolute or relative private real income. For a negative income tax to have this effect it must first deliver to the present poor and near poor a larger money income than existing welfare schemes. Whether this larger money income will turn out to a larger real income needs investigation.

A negative income tax or social dividend scheme that is an instrument in an effort to eliminate poverty will

(1) set a substantially higher floor to family money incomes than now exists,
(2) set an effective marginal income tax rate, on even the lowest tax code incomes, that is substantially higher than the existing marginal income tax rates on tax code incomes as large or even larger than the break-even income, and
(3) deliver net benefits, as measured by disposable money income, to households that have tax code incomes that are well above the poverty line, however it may be defined.

In addition, the benefits will be by right (no means tests), and will be responsive to changing circumstances. There will be no substantial lags or costs in getting on or off the benefit-receiving status as earned income or family status changes.

Points (2) and (3) are related. They show that a trade-off exists between the numbers for whom the substitution ratio between leisure and work is changed by the higher tax rate and the size of the change. The higher the marginal tax rate for a given income floor, the lower the upper limit to incomes that receive net benefits. That is, a $3,000 floor to income and a 50 percent tax rate on tax code income will lead to a $6,000 ceiling to incomes that receive net benefits; with the same minimum, a $33.\overline{3}$ percent tax rate yields a $9,000 ceiling to incomes that receive net benefits.

The higher the tax rate, the greater the substitution effect upon each impacted household, i.e., the greater the stimulus to substitute leisure for work. The lower the tax rate, the greater the number for whom a rise in the marginal tax rate occurs; the greater the number for whom the stimulus to substitute leisure for work has increased. As the distribution of income from work is roughly bell shaped, a decrease in the tax rate on earned income will lead to a relatively large increase in the number for whom there exists a positive disincentive effect due to higher taxes, as long as the break-even income is not greatly in excess of the median income. The choice is between a large disincentive effect on a relatively few or a smaller disincentive effect on many.

Welfare schemes which offset earned income by equivalent decreases in welfare benefits are, in effect, a 100 percent tax on earned income. This maximizes the disincentive per unit affected, but it minimizes the size of the impacted population. Small social dividends which can be financed without any rise in the tax schedule (as a result of the so-called fiscal dividend) will not affect the substitution ratio between work and leisure, except as it is an alternative to lowering tax rates on earned income.

The additional point about administrative responsiveness and ease means that the negative income tax scheme becomes a guarantee of a minimum cash flow per period to each household.

The negative income tax is but one example of a welfare scheme. It is unique in that it provides a floor to money income as a right and combines the floor to income with a tax on earned income that is substantially higher, for both low incomes and incomes in the neighborhood of the median, than now rule. Some of what holds for the negative income tax holds for all schemes that attempt to affect the distribution of income by transfers and taxes, including schemes which provide income in kind, such as Medicare. Some of what holds, such as the implications of higher marginal taxes on earned income, are special to the particular set of schemes.

In designing [and] evaluating a welfare scheme, or any other scheme, allowance must be made for its systemic as well as its direct or primary efforts. This means that a model of the economy must be set up and the various functions of the model must be modified to allow for the scheme. Once this is done, the differences in

The Macroeconomics of a Negative Income Tax (1969)

behavior or properties of the model with the unchanged and the modified functions can be determined.

In order to determine the macroeconomic effects of a negative income tax, it will be assumed that an income–expenditure model that explicitly incorporates uncertainty is a good description of the economy.[4] Thus the negative income tax will be assumed to have implications for consumption, investment, and portfolio behavior, as well as for the supply of labor.

In addition to the assumptions about the impact of the change in the welfare schemes upon the functions of the macroeconomic model, it is necessary to make some assumptions about the policy goals. This is so because, if the macroeconomic effects of a negative income tax initially lead to undesired changes in variables that are other policy objectives, action taken in an attempt to achieve the other policy goals may erode the effect of the negative income tax.

It will be shown that a negative income tax is expansionary or inflationary, even if budgets are balanced. Monetary and fiscal constraint can offset this inflationary pressure, but at a cost in the measured gross national product and rate of growth. If measured gross national product or its rate of growth is a policy goal, then general monetary and fiscal constraint is not available. There exists a price level at which the real value of the negative income tax equals the real value of the prior welfare schemes. If distributional details are ignored, at this price level the pre–negative income tax equilibrium is reestablished. However, the distributional details cannot be ignored. If the negative income tax induces inflation, there will be an upward shift in tax code incomes. Families which initially were net beneficiaries would cross the break-even line in dollar terms and experience a decline in their real income. Simultaneously, the rise in prices will erode the real value of the benefits to the poor. The end result will be an equilibrium which delivers less in real terms than promised to the poor, while biting more deeply than anticipated into the real income of the not-poor, but not very well-off, population.

As the negative income tax is but one example of a welfare system change, what is true about the expansionary and inflationary effects is true about any significant improvement in the welfare system. The postwar economic history of Britain, with its relatively slow rate of growth, in part may be due to the combination of an expansionary (inflationary) stimulus of the welfare scheme and the existence of a balance-of-payments constraint. The recent inflationary pressure in the United States, and the resistance of the inflation to monetary and fiscal constraint, followed upon substantial increases in Social Security, the introduction of Medicare, and improvements in the welfare system associated with the War on Poverty.

The lesson to be learned from this exercise is that system-wide as well as direct effects must be considered in evaluating public policy instruments. System-wide repercussions can offset, in all or in part, the direct effects of a policy action and in addition impose unintended costs or losses. It is obvious from what follows that a negative income tax generous enough to significantly reduce or eliminate poverty will have many repercussions. It is shown that these system effects tend to offset at least part of the initial benefits to the poor and may impose unintended real costs upon families with modest incomes.

Impact Points of a Negative Income Tax

There is no need to quibble over the specifics of the program. For our example of a meaningful negative income tax, a standard family of four is assumed to receive a $3,000 social dividend and to pay a $33.\bar{3}$ percent tax on the first $15,000 of tax code income. For tax code incomes greater than this the marginal tax rate will be unchanged at $33.\bar{3}$ percent or more. With this scheme every family making less than $9,000 a year is better off. If we assume that the rate on [the] $9,000–$15,000 tax bracket was 25 percent prior to and $33.\bar{3}$ after the tax, then for those making in excess of $15,000, a $500 decrease in disposable income will occur; for those between $9,000 and $15,000, the decrease in disposable income will be a proportional part of the $500. If this tax does not gather enough to pay for the negative tax payments, then it will be necessary to add some percentage points to the tax schedule either to all incomes or perhaps only to those above the break-even income level.

The Macroeconomics of a Negative Income Tax (1969)

It is assumed, perhaps heroically, that the negative income tax would not by itself throw the government's budget out of balance at full employment. That is, the increase in the marginal tax rates on earned income above the break-even level as well as the funds released from existing welfare schemes will fully pay for the program. Thus, initially, we conceive of the scheme as a transfer, where the sum of cash benefits equals the sum of taxes paid on account of the scheme and the funds released from other schemes.

An effective negative income tax will have three direct effects:

1. an income and a substitution effect operating through the supply of labor function,
2. a wealth effect operating through the consumption function, and
3. a cash-flow effect operating through the liquidity preference function.

As a result of the impact upon the liquidity preference function, the amount of investment can be expected to change. In addition to the extent that entrepreneurial expectations as to how the economy will function are affected by the negative income tax, there will be an effect upon the investment function.

An effective negative income tax will increase the disposable income of those earning less than the break-even income, lower the marginal tax rate on the welfare poor, and raise the marginal tax rate on income from work for the working poor as well as for families in the neighborhood of the break-even income.

Presumably, an income effect due to the higher minimum income guarantees will tend to induce withdrawals from the labor force. The marginal tax rate on the welfare poor will be reduced from 100 percent, as in present welfare schemes, to the rate in the negative income tax scheme. This will tend to increase labor force participation. Thus, there will be some offsetting tendencies on the labor offered by the very-low-income population and the welfare poor that will follow from the substitution of a negative income tax for the present welfare schemes. As an aside, it is worth noting that a reduction of the tax rate on earned income for the welfare poor could be obtained without any of the other features of the negative income tax proposals. Since this 100 percent tax aspect of welfare schemes has been pointed out, some welfare schemes have been modified to eliminate this feature.

A negative income tax will raise the marginal tax rate on income from work for families well up in the income scale. Many families with heads of household working full time will simultaneously experience a rise in disposable income combined with a rise in the marginal tax rate. Using our standard example of the tax scheme, a household earning $6,000 a year of tax code income will have a disposable income of $7,000. If the household "feels" that a $6,000 disposable income is adequate, it can achieve this by reducing its labor market participation so as to earn $4,500 a year of tax code income.

A significant portion of total labor used is from second wage earners in families, overtime, and moonlighting (second jobs). Even if the basic workweek labor, mainly supplied by heads of households, is not affected by such a tax, the willingness of women to take on part-time work (Christmas, etc.) and for the head of the household to work overtime or moonlight will be affected. Thus, for the large group of families clustered below and around the median, the tendency will be to substitute leisure for income as a result of the lower net return from work.

It is worth noting that leisure as measured by not participating in the labor force may be more valuable to households with adequate incomes and some property than to those with low incomes and no property. Much of recreation presupposes income. But, in addition, not participating in the labor force need not imply idleness. Do-it-yourself is a way of supplementing tax code income by income in kind. Such income is most available to households with some property; for example, the improvement of an owned home by sweat capital.

Experimental attempts to measure the disincentive effects of a negative income tax are highly desirable (Orcutt and Orcutt 1968). However, studies which examine the reaction of very-low-income workers may miss what can be the most important labor market

The Macroeconomics of a Negative Income Tax (1969)

participation effect of such proposals: the withdrawal of some labor from families already represented in the labor force whose incomes are well above the poverty level. Behavioral assumptions made by those with high incomes, whose very job yields "income" in kind, and tested on those with very low incomes may have little predictive validity for the behavior of the largest group affected by a negative income tax, those whose incomes are clustered around and just below the median incomes.

Labor supplied can be considered to be a function of the real wage, real nonhuman capital, and the real capitalized present value of the welfare system. At any moment the welfare system's benefits are fixed in money terms. If we posit a capitalization ratio K applicable to the nominal benefits from the welfare system E, then the real capitalized value of the welfare system is $\frac{KE}{p}$, where p is the price level appropriate to the standard of life of the impacted population. The labor supply function is

(1) $N_s = N_s\left(\frac{W}{p}, V, \frac{KE}{p}\right)$, where N_s is the labor supply, W the money wage, p the price level, V the real market value of nonhuman wealth, and $\frac{KE}{p}$ the capitalized value of the welfare system. From the above arguments we would expect that $\frac{\alpha N_s}{\alpha(\frac{KE}{p})} < 0$; we also have that $\frac{\alpha N_s}{\alpha(\frac{W}{p})} > 0$ and $\frac{\alpha N_s}{\alpha V} < 0$.

If effective, a negative income tax raises the floor to real income for all families which do not have a substantial net worth. Given a family's income [and] human and nonhuman wealth, and taking the economic and demographic position of the family into account, there exist contingencies under which their current disposable income and income in kind would, in whole or in part, be due to the welfare system. The value of these welfare receipts under the existing law times the "subjective" likelihood of the various contingencies occurring, discounted back to this date at some appropriate interest rate, gives the present value of the welfare system to a household. Households not on welfare—or not even receiving net benefits from the negative income tax—are made better off by the existence of such protection against even unlikely contingencies.

This is so because the typical household is a risk averter and the welfare scheme is in the nature of "free" insurance policy. Certainty of income at the minimum level or certainty of supplements on the occurrence of contingencies is, for risk averters, the equivalent of an increase in present wealth.[5]

A meaningful negative income tax will raise the present value of the welfare system substantially for the poor and the near poor. If the likelihood of unemployment or short time is taken into account, a large portion of workers experience such impoverishing events over a four-to-five-year period. Such families will be better off by some substantial amount as a result of the higher floor to disposable income; i.e., the capitalized value of the improved welfare scheme will be a substantial portion of the family's nonhuman wealth.

Many studies have shown that wealth—human and nonhuman—affects the [ratio of consumption to current or measured income]: the higher the wealth or permanent income for a given level of actual income, the greater the consumption level.[6] An improvement in the system of welfare payments by, in effect, increasing wealth can be expected to raise the consumption–measured income ratio of all except those at the very highest incomes.

Consumption expenditures can be considered to be a function of income, real nonhuman wealth, the interest rate, and the real capitalized value of the welfare scheme. That is, the consumption function is

(2) $C = C(Y, V, r, \frac{KE}{P})$, where C is consumption, Y income, and r the interest rate. We expect that $\frac{\alpha C}{\alpha(\frac{KE}{P})} > 0$; we also expect $\frac{\alpha C}{\alpha Y} > 0$, $\frac{\alpha C}{\alpha V} > 0$, and $\frac{\alpha C}{\alpha r} < 0$.

If the cash flows from labor and property are susceptible to reduction due to economic or life cycle events, a household, if rational, will hold some precautionary balances of liquid or cash assets. The introduction of a negative income tax will mean that for many units a substantially higher minimum cash flow per period will be guaranteed than was true prior to the tax. Thus precautionary holdings of cash and near-cash assets can be decreased. The affected households can reduce their liquidity either by going into more adventurous financial assets or by purchasing consumers' capital goods.

The Macroeconomics of a Negative Income Tax (1969)

This portfolio transformation will mean that the average cash and near-cash balance per dollar of income and of other assets will decrease. Independently of any expansion in the money supply, aggregate money demand will increase as a negative income tax is introduced. In the conventional language of economics the guarantees embodied in an effective negative income tax will tend to increase velocity.

The liquidity preference function, interpreted as a demand for money, can be considered as a function of money income, the interest rate, the money value of the capital stock, and the money value of the welfare system. Thus we can write

(3) $M_D = L(Y_p, r, V_p, KE)$ and $\frac{\alpha M_D}{\alpha KE} < 0$; we also have that $\frac{\alpha M_D}{\alpha Y_p} > 0$, $\frac{\alpha M_D}{\alpha r} < 0$, and $\frac{\alpha M_D}{\alpha V_p} > 0$.

A change in welfare laws that raises the capitalized value of welfare will not have a direct effect upon investment. An improvement in welfare will reduce the demand for money balances and thus will tend to lower interest rates. This in turn will tend to raise investment.

The impact that an improvement in welfare will have upon [the] labor supply can be expected to induce a substitution of capital for labor in production, thus generating an increase in investment demand.

These system impacts upon investment will, however, be smaller than the effect upon investment that can follow from any change in the expectational climate that may follow upon the improvements in welfare. It will be argued that the labor supply and the consumption function shifts, together with the facilitating effects upon the demand for money, will induce an inflationary expansion. As this becomes apparent, speculative shifts in the investment and liquidity preference functions will take place.

It should be noted that no quantitative estimates of these various impacts exist and it is quite likely that some of the effects will be small. However, they all operate in the same expansionary-inflationary direction, and it is the combined or cumulative effect that is at issue. [. . .]*

Distributional and Policy Goal Effects

A negative income tax will affect many facets of system behavior. Therefore it is necessary to distinguish between the actual and the intended result of such a change. A negative income tax is adopted to change the distribution of income in a particular way. Changes in money disposable income, as stated by the law, are at least implicitly taken to be changes in real income. As a result of the system-wide effects that follow from the introduction of a negative income tax, the actual changes in the distribution of income will be different from those intended.

The introduction of a negative income tax in a full employment economy is inflationary. As benefits and tax rates are set in money terms, inflation erodes their real value. As the inflationary thrust dies out, a new equilibrium is reached. Its characteristics need to be known.

Price stability may be a major or overriding policy goal, perhaps because of a commitment to fixed exchange rates. Monetary and fiscal policy may be used to offset the inflationary tendencies. The new equilibrium with these policy goals needs to be determined.

Distributional Effects

The introduction of a meaningful negative income tax shifts the consumption and liquidity preference functions so that excess aggregate demand appears. Simultaneously, the labor supply function shifts so that labor supplied by families with incomes in the neighborhood of the median decreases at the same time as labor supplied by welfare families increases. If no explicit offsetting steps are taken, an inflationary expansion will take place. What will be the nature of the equilibrium after the inflationary pressures are exhausted? The possibility of an investment boom, with the result that business cycles are triggered, is ignored.

---

*See Appendix to this chapter for a model of the impacts (located here in the original manuscript.)

The Macroeconomics of a Negative Income Tax (1969)

Initially, benefits in the form of increases in disposable income and the valuable assurance of a minimum income are widespread. Only families which have high incomes and substantial net worth are worse off, and this is a conscious policy choice. Even so, our model scheme has a maximum to the decline in money income for a family ($500 in the example).

As money wages rise, families pass from being net beneficiaries to being net taxpayers. As prices rise, the real value of the transfers and the insurance features declines, as does the real value of the maximum additional tax any household pays.

Let us assume that initially the budget is balanced and throughout the inflationary period the budget for items other than the negative income tax remains balanced. The decline in benefits and the increase in receipts on account of the negative income tax that accompanies the rise in wages means that a surplus develops, and this surplus increases as long as wages rise.

Both the rise in prices and in wage incomes erodes the real benefits of the negative income tax. As a result, the labor supply consumption and liquidity preference functions drift back toward their initial position, therefore increasing aggregate supply and decreasing aggregate demand. The emerging surplus also tends to decrease demand. Excess aggregate demand will be eliminated before inflation completely wipes out the distributional effect of the negative income tax. There will be some residual improvement in the income of the lowest income groups and the protection embodied in the law will still be worth something to some proportion of the population with incomes in the neighborhood of the old median income. However, families who initially took the maximum possible decline in nominal income will find that the decline in real income is smaller than anticipated.

Inasmuch as the initial change is only partially eroded by the inflation, only part of the initial decline in aggregate supply will be offset. The initial impact upon liquidity preference will tend to increase investment; the initial impact upon consumption will tend to decrease investment. A priori, it is not possible to argue which dominates; this depends upon the behavior of the investment function and the way in which other policy instruments are used. It is best to examine the impact upon the rate of growth in the context of an examination of policy goals.

Price Stability

If a negative income tax sets off inflationary pressures and if the ultimate equilibrium is characterized by (1) the poor receiving a positive net benefit smaller than intended, (2) a larger group of losers than intended, and (3) a budgetary surplus, then a more modest negative income tax combined with a planned budget surplus could have achieved the same real result without the price increases. The more generous the negative income tax scheme, the greater the required surplus; thus, in principle there exists a tax scheme such that real transfers can be as large as desired. However, higher tax rates mean greater withdrawals from the labor market. The possibility exists that the rise in tax rates may have a greater effect in reducing supply than in reducing demand: a maximum to the amount that can be transferred exists.

For inflation to exist in spite of fiscal constraint, monetary ease is necessary. The impact of a negative income tax upon the liquidity preference function is conducive to monetary ease. Thus an offsetting constraint in the rate of growth of money is necessary. This implies high interest rates and a low rate of investment.

If we recognize that the price stability goal is often the byproduct of a balance-of-payments constraint, and if we assume that there is some limit to the fiscal constraint that can be operative, then a considerable part of the anti-inflationary burden needs to be carried by monetary policy. This implies that investment is constrained, which in turn implies a low rate of growth.

Conclusions

The negative income tax has been proposed as an effective, straightforward weapon for the eradication of poverty. It is in truth a complex instrument, and its use may lead to unintended and undesirable side effects. In particular, a negative income tax may tend to induce inflation, reduce measured gross national product, and lower the measured rate of growth of the economy. As the induced inflation works its way through the economy, the real disposable income of families with quite modest incomes will decline and the net benefits to the intended beneficiaries will be eroded.

These repercussions follow from the higher marginal tax rates on quite modest incomes leading to a withdrawal of some labor from the market and from the value of the guarantees embodied in the scheme to families that may not directly benefit, inducing increased consumption and more adventuresome portfolios. Whether the induced inflation will be rapid and large or slow and small is not known and would be difficult to estimate. If the induced inflation is slow and small, and if one believes that experience with higher real incomes will integrate the present disadvantaged and poor into society, then the undesirable side effects can perhaps be endured. If the net gains to the present poor evaporate quickly and almost completely, and if the residual gain of the poor is mainly at the expense of the slightly better-off, then the costs of a negative income tax might far outweigh its benefits.

It is worth noting that the macroeconomic effects of previous improvements in welfare systems have not been adequately studied. Britain experienced a large rise in its welfare and social services system after World War II. The past 20 years have been years of inflationary pressures and slow growth. The improvement in welfare schemes in the United States following the election of 1964 ushered in a period of price inflation which has proven to be resistant to monetary and fiscal measures. Of course, other events such as Britain's wartime debts and the Vietnam War have been factors in creating these situations.

However, the general point of the argument is valid: far-reaching schemes must be subject to a critical examination in order to ascertain their system-wide effects, and all too often schemes which have general, system-wide effects are adopted and examined on the assumption that they have only local, particular effects. The design and evaluation of policy instruments must take into account both the direct impact upon the problem being attacked and system-wide effects. In this paper it has been argued that the system-wide effects of a negative income tax are such as to cast doubts as to its ability to deliver the benefits claimed for the scheme.

Appendix: System Behavior

A number of models of increasing complexity will be used to show how a negative income tax can be expected to affect system behavior. These models will assume that there are policy goals, which can be stated in terms of the level of measured real gross national product or the rate of growth of real gross national product in addition to the "goal" expressed in the welfare scheme. In a later section the implications of a policy goal of price stability will be examined.

1. Labor Demand and Supply

Let us assume a target real gross national product as the policy goal. For simplicity, output produced is a function of labor employed. At a given money wage, W_0, target aggregate demand is transformed into an elastic demand for labor:

(4) $N_D = \bar{N}_D(\frac{\bar{Y}}{p}, W_0)$ where N_D = labor demand and $\frac{\bar{Y}}{p}$ is the target real gross national product. The price level is a mark up on the money wage rate

(5) $p = \lambda W_0$ with $\lambda > 1$. At the initial value of the welfare scheme labor supply equals labor demand

(6) $N_S = N_D$, i.e., $\bar{N}_D((\frac{\bar{Y}}{p}), W_0) = N_S\left(\frac{W_0}{p}, \bar{V}, \frac{KE}{p}\right)$ so that

(7) $W_0 = Q(\bar{Y}, \lambda, \bar{V}, \bar{KE}_0)$ where ⁻ indicates initial values which do not change over the period; E_0 is the initial money value of the welfare scheme.

An improvement in the welfare scheme which raises its real present value reduces the labor supply. At W_0 as determined in equation (7), $N_D > N_S$, i.e., excess demand for labor appears. This implies rising money wages, which in turn means rising prices. Real wages do not rise. Rising wages and prices reduce the real value of the welfare scheme. There exists a price level such that the real value of the welfare scheme is back at its original value. At the wage rate corresponding to this price level the initial equilibrium is reestablished. With a facilitating monetary system, a target level

The Macroeconomics of a Negative Income Tax (1969)

of real gross national product, and a fiscal system (excluding the welfare system) that is fixed in real terms, any improvement in the welfare system must be inflated out.

2. Consumption and Growth

The impact of a negative income tax on consumption can be divided into two parts: the first due to a rise in transfer payments to low-income groups, the second due to the wealth effect of the legislation.

It is assumed that the budget remains balanced even though welfare transfers are increased. Thus taxes offset the transfer payments. The rise in present value or the disposable income of the actual benefit recipients are offset by an equal decline for the actual taxpayers. It is also assumed that there is no net distribution effect upon consumption: the gains in consumption by the actual recipients offset the decline by net taxpayers.

However, in addition to the actual transfer payments there is a net gain from the insurance policy absorption of uncertainty aspects of the scheme. If we write the consumption function

(8) $C = C(Y, V, r, \frac{KE}{P}, E_t, T_t)$, E, and T_t being the tth periods benefits and taxes, and $E_t = T_t$ for all t it is nevertheless true that $\frac{dC}{dE} > 0$, i.e., an equal rise in welfare payments and taxes will raise consumption. This is so because $\frac{d(\frac{KE}{P})}{dE} > 0$ for the increased security that the larger transfer provides decreases the incentives to save.

Let us ignore the labor supply impact of a negative income tax — thus current income remains target income and no price pressures exist due to excess demand for labor. Let us for the moment assume investment exogenously determined. An upward shift of the consumption function will increase aggregate demand — and at current prices aggregate demand will exceed aggregate supply.

In a simple classical model a shift of this sort in the consumption function will raise the interest rate and, assuming the correct shapes, raise consumption and lower investment. The unchanged gross national product will be split differently between consumption and investment.

However, if the rate of growth of output is a policy goal, then the decline in investment will lead to a decline in the rate of growth. The policy goal of growth means that an attempt will be made to finance and put in place an unchanged amount of real investment. This implies an excess demand for both output and labor. Wage and price increases will erode the value of the welfare scheme in nominal terms. Thus an equilibrating process tending to inflate out the rise in the welfare schemes will take place. Equilibrium at the old real value of the insurance aspects of welfare will be reached.

Both the consumption and the labor supply impacts of a rise in welfare schemes tend to generate an excess demand for labor and wage and price increases. Thus we can assert that if $\left(\frac{KE_0}{P_0}\right)$ was consistent with equilibrium in both markets and $E_1 > E_0$ is introduced, then there exists a p_1 such that $\left(\frac{KE_0}{P_0}\right) = \left(\frac{KE_1}{P_1}\right)$, which makes E_1 consistent with the simultaneous equilibrium in the two markets. The market disequilibria set up where the schemes are introduced will tend to generate price movement toward p_1.

3. Liquidity Preference and the Financing of Excess Demand

The introduction of a negative income tax is equivalent to introducing in all portfolios a fully paid-up insurance policy which sets a floor to cash receipts. For families, including many now well above the median income, this floor is considerably higher than the minimum assured cash flow without the negative income tax. Adjustments will be undertaken in the light of this addition to portfolio.

At existing asset prices families will now have excess supplies of cash and near-cash assets and too little in the way of business and household real or equity investments. In addition, the larger assured cash flow will make households willing to emit liabilities that commit future cash flows and to use the funds so raised to purchase real household assets and equity-type financial assets. Thus a spillover via portfolio adjustments to investment exists.

The larger assured minimum cash flow will increase the attractiveness of such household liabilities to financial intermediaries.

A negative income tax interpreted as a portfolio change is expansionary. In conjunction with the impact that a negative income tax has upon consumption and the labor supply, this means that the excess aggregate demand can be financed. It is not necessary for the monetary and fiscal authorities to be accommodating; it is sufficient if they are passive: an improvement in the welfare system tends to increase velocity.

If equilibrium in the labor, commodity, and money markets existed at an initial price level and value of the welfare system, and if the capitalized value of the improvements in the welfare system as it affects the labor supply, consumption, and liquidity preference system is the same, then there exists a new price level such that the real value of the augmented welfare system equals the real value of the initial welfare system.

4. Investment and Expectations

A spillover from the portfolio relation to the price of the stock of real (and equity) assets, and thus to the demand price for investment, has been noted. In addition, the portfolio impact will tend to make the terms upon which new investment can be financed more favorable. Thus with an unchanged investment function, the amount of investment put into place can be expected to increase. Imbedded in the positioning of the investment function is the expectational climate. If changes in the expectational climate can be expected to follow upon the introduction of a negative income tax, this indirect effect upon the investment function can have a greater effect than that by way of financing terms and demand prices for investment.

If a negative income tax leads to a significant rise in the floor to real income, it will imply a rise in the minimum expected consumption levels. In addition, investment tends to respond positively to inflationary expectations. If inflationary pressures begin to be observed, investment will tend to respond positively. Thus the improved real prospects and the price-level expectations that can be expected to follow a negative income tax will tend to shift the investment function "upward."

5. Conclusion

By itself, unless countermeasures are taken, the introduction of a negative income tax will tend to generate inflationary pressures. It can be shown, under rather strict assumptions, that such pressures will continue as long as the welfare system's real value is greater than its initial or equilibrium real value. Thus the improvement in the welfare system will be inflated out.

If we assume that there are no distributional effects, then the end result will be a welfare floor to income no greater than the initial floor; however, distributional effects exist. Even if the real value of the welfare system returns to its initial value, it does not necessarily follow that the value of the welfare system to the poor and the near poor returns to its initial value. However, to the extent that there are residual benefits to the poor, there will be costs imposed upon other groups which differ from the costs initially imposed by the tax scheme. Thus distributional effects and the effects of relaxing the policy goals need to be considered.

Notes

1. Christopher Green (1967) examines various negative income tax and social dividend proposals. Peter Diamond (1968) reviews Green's book and examines the labor market disincentive effects of negative income taxes.
2. The various suggestions run from a low minimum of $1,500 (Friedman and Lampman*) to a high minimum of $3,200 (Yale plan). For a description of Friedman's and Lampman's plans see Vadakin (1968). The Yale scheme takes the form of a model tax law; see Yale Law Journal (1968).
3. It is possible to favor a negative income tax on the general philosophical ground that the decision maker in each household knows best how to maximize the satisfaction received from the resources available to it. Thus the provision of income in kind to both the poor and the nonpoor is objectionable—whether the income in kind be schools, medical care, subsidized housing, or services of the police, courts, and fire departments. Such market anarchism ignores or minimizes the significance of externalities, such as my being better off if your children are both vaccinated and educated, and the existence of community—or civilized—standards, so one would gladly sacrifice one's private consumption for another's safety on the street. The arguments for the maximum of such "freedom" as well as a recognition of some of its limits are in M. Friedman (1967) and Simons (1948).
4. Any standard textbook on macroeconomics, such as Ackley (1961), has an exposition of the basic model. Fundamentally, the class of models builds on J. Hicks,

---

* Milton Friedman and Robert Lampman.

"Mr. Keynes and the 'Classics': A Suggested Interpretation," originally published in *Econometrica* (1937) and since reprinted in many volumes.

Recently, the validity of this view of the Keynesian model has been questioned by Clower (1965), Leijonhufvud (1968), and Minsky (1969).

For the meaning of uncertainty in the context of Keynesian economics see Keynes (1936, chapter 17; 1937).

5. For the economics of risk aversion and the impact of uncertainty upon the organization of activity see Friedman and Savage (1948), and Arrow (1963; 1965). Diamond (1968) examines the impact of a negative income tax on saving via its effect upon uncertainty.

6. Note that the consumption function does not include a real balance effect, i.e., $V \neq \frac{K_p}{P} + \frac{M}{P}$, where M is the amount of outside money in existence. Such an effect could be introduced but it would be irrelevant to our basic problem. For an exposition of the real balance effect see Patinkin (1965). The models examined here can be interpreted as treating the welfare system's impact upon consumption in a way that is analogous to Patinkin's treatment of money.

Sources

Ackley, G. 1961. *Macroeconomic Theory*. New York: Macmillan.

Arrow, K. 1963. "Uncertainty and the Welfare Economics of Medical Care." *The American Economic Review* 53(5): 941–73.

———. 1965. "Aspects of the Theory of Risk Bearing." Yrjö Jahnsson Lectures. Yrjö Jahnssonin Säätiö, Helsinki.

Clower, R. W. 1965. "The Keynesian Counterrevolution: A Theoretical Appraisal." In F. H. Hahn and F. D. R. Brechling, eds. *The Theory of Interest Rates*, 103–25. New York: Macmillan.

Diamond, P. 1968. "Negative Taxes and the Poverty Problem. A Review Article." *National Tax Journal* 21(3): 288–302.

Friedman, M. 1967. *Capitalism and Freedom*. Chicago: University of Chicago Press.

Friedman, M., and L. J. Savage. 1948. "The Utility Analysis of Choices Involving Risk." *Journal of Political Economy* 56(4): 279–304.

Green, C. 1967. "Negative Taxes and the Poverty Problem." Washington, D.C.: The Brookings Institution.

Hicks, J. R. 1937. "Mr. Keynes and the 'Classics'; A Suggested Interpretation." *Econometrica* 5(2): 147–59.

Keynes, J. M. 1936. *The General Theory of Employment, Interest and Money*. New York: Harcourt, Brace.

———. 1937. "The General Theory of Employment." *The Quarterly Journal of Economics* 51(2): 209–23.

Leijonhufvud, A. 1968. *On Keynesian Economics and the Economics of Keynes*. New York: Oxford University Press.

Minsky, H. P. 1969. "Private Sector Asset Management and the Effectiveness of Monetary Policy: Theory and Practice." *The Journal of Finance* 24(2): 223–38.

Patinkin, D. 1965. *Money, Interest, and Prices*. 2nd ed. New York: Harper and Row.

Orcutt, G. H., and A. G. Orcutt. 1968. "Incentive and Disincentive Experimentation for Income Maintenance Policy Purposes." *The American Economic Review* 58(4): 754–72.

Simons, H. 1948. "A Positive Program for Laissez-Faire: Some Proposals for a Liberal Economic Policy." In *Economic Policy for a Free Society*, 40–77. Chicago: University of Chicago Press.

Vadakin, J. C. 1968. "A Critique of the Guaranteed Annual Income." *The Public Interest*, no. 11, (Spring): 55–66.

Yale Law Journal. 1968. "A Model Negative Income Tax Statute." *The Yale Law Journal* 78(2): 269–337.

Chapter 5

Where the American Economy—and Economists—Went Wrong* (1972)

Introduction

An oppressive malaise is abroad in the United States. This is only superficially due to the unending war, the persisting inflation joined to high unemployment, and the unappealing nature of recent presidents. By the usual economic indices—the growth of GNP and the absence of a serious depression—the times are quite good. By indices of a political-economic nature, such as the overt and wide dissatisfaction with and resentment of the way in which the economy distributes its benefits and burdens, and the justified feeling that the politicians and their intellectuals do not have the answers to our problems, the times are truly bad.

Today's crisis is not the result of the uncontrollable and inevitable working of nature: our plight is largely man-made. We have just come off of more than a decade of unprecedented activism in economic policy. The confident and often arrogant house economists of the Kennedy, Johnson, and Nixon regimes announced that they knew what our targets should be and that they had the capacity to control and guide—nay, fine-tune—the economy so as to hit the targets. They both defined the nation's priorities and manipulated policy instruments as their theory dictated. Our present plight is the result.

We should not underestimate the power of house intellectuals. As Professor Tobin of Yale, who served Kennedy and now advises McGovern[†] wrote, "the terms in which a problem is stated and in which the relevant information is organized can have a great influence on its solution" (Tobin 1966, 14). A political leader is a captive of his house intellectuals and they in turn are prisoners of their theories—of their intellectual baggage.

---

* Revised text of a talk prepared for delivery at Southern Illinois University, Carbondale, May 20, 1971. Paper 428 ("Third Version"). Hyman P. Minsky Archive, Levy Economics Institute, Annandale-on-Hudson, N.Y.

[†] George McGovern, 1972 US presidential nominee for the Democratic Party.

During the past three administrations a special brand of economic theory—the neoclassical synthesis—has been the intellectual baggage of the economists who have acted as policy advisers. Much of what is wrong with the American economy is due to the "tilt" that this theory has given to economic policy. This neoclassical synthesis is not only responsible for where we are but it cannot, because of the way in which sets up problems, serve as a guide to the resolution of our current crisis.

The economic root of our malaise is that even though we have succeeded in preventing serious depressions and in assuring that growth in measured GNP takes place, we have failed miserably in those dimensions of our economy that determine the quality of life. Our cities and our suburbs are in shambles, and our rural society has been well-nigh liquidated. Public services and the services from vital organizations such as hospitals and utilities have deteriorated. The landscape and the environment have been despoiled. A crescendo of violence and fear has accompanied what passes for prosperity and growth. Civil behavior, rights, and liberties are apparent victims of our economic progress. It has become obvious to all that the highly touted success of the economy depends upon a debilitating addition to military spending and adventures. In many ways poverty has spread even as GNP has grown. Above all, the fairness of the system is now in question. "Perhaps American capitalism is efficient, however, it most certainly is not equitable" seems to be the judgment of the 1970s.

Today's dominant economic need is not more but better. The vital questions are for what, for whom, and how shall our economic capabilities be used. Vast amounts of resources are used to induce waste; we are locked into myths such as a "housing shortage" when entire neighborhoods of good housing are being abandoned. The need is for equity and justice to dominate narrow efficiency and growth as the goals of economic life. Social objectives and, if a pun will be pardoned, the humane society are now more important than increasing private wealth.

Three aspects of the neoclassical synthesis—the narrow definition of income and objectives, the technological treatment of income

Where the American Economy—and Economists—Went Wrong (1972)

distribution, and the abstraction from capitalist finance—are mainly responsible for the bias given by economic theory to economic policies that led to today's crisis.

Our malaise is deep because it reflects the failure of both an ideal and a dominant theory. The American dream—that private economic success, measured in terms of ever more private goods, is all that is needed for a person and for a nation—has collapsed. The theory which rationalized that dream and gave us policies to realize it has proven to be irrelevant as new problems of the economy arise. Our theory and our dominant intellectuals have lost both their power to impress and their capacity to lead.

Thus an intellectual vacuum and real problems coexist. Keynes, in the famous closing passage to *The General Theory*, wrote, "At the present moment people are unusually expectant of a more fundamental diagnosis; more particularly ready to receive it; eager to try it out, if it should be even plausible. But apart from this contemporary mood, the ideas of economists and political philosophers, both when they are right and when they are wrong, are more powerful than is commonly understood. Indeed the world is ruled by little else" (Keynes 1964 [1936], 383).

The 1970s are like the 1930s. Once again, to meet the problems of an economic crisis it is necessary to search out new directions in economic theory.

An Aside on the Neoclassical Synthesis

The neoclassical synthesis is the current standard economic theory. It is a blend of Walras-Pareto general equilibrium theory designed to generate rules for efficiency, and Keynesian income and employment theory designed to establish rules for controlling business cycles. It guides the thinking of well-nigh all the publicly prominent economists in the United States, the leading exception being Professor Galbraith.[*]

This system of thought is based upon two fundamental analytical constructs: preference systems which embody households'

---

[*] John Kenneth Galbraith.

subjective valuations of commodities, and resources and production functions which embody the techniques open to firms. Preference systems rank "bundles of goods" and can be "revealed" in markets by the way income is spent. Production functions give us the technology of the economy—they describe how firms can combine inputs—labor, materials, and machine time—to yield outputs.

In the Walras-Pareto theory each household is assigned some initial endowment. Trading takes place. Each household is assumed to trade only if the trade makes it better off, or at least no worse off. Some of the trades will result in furnishing services (labor) to production units; some will be exchanges of commodities.

From these preference systems, production functions, and initial endowments, supply and demand curves for labor and outputs of various kinds are derived. Equilibrium exists when supply equals demand for every variety of labor and output. Trading processes are defined so that such an equilibrium will be achieved and the shapes of preference and production functions are specified so that this equilibrium will be stable. This equilibrium will be at full employment—or at a natural rate of unemployment. It is now usual to set the model up so that it will generate a growing economy.

This framework leads to a mathematical, rigorous proof that under restrictive conditions, the equivalent of Adam Smith's invisible hand proposition—that each by serving his own interest serves the social good—is true: efficiency is served by avarice. The conditions required for this formal proof are sufficiently restrictive so that this result can be interpreted as showing that the model is or that it is not relevant to our economy.

The Keynesian component of the neoclassical synthesis yields the proposition that equilibrium at less than full employment is possible. The analysis begins by investigating how the private components of aggregate demand—consumption and investment—are determined. In the standard presentations of the neoclassical synthesis these demands are derived from preference systems and production functions. Keynes emphasized that capital holding and investment decisions are speculative and as a result investment is volatile and cannot be explained by productivity and thrift. In the

Keynesian part of the neoclassical synthesis it is assumed that, due to either the volatility of investors' views of the world or the inducements or constraints flowing from the monetary and fiscal system, consumption demand plus investment demand can add up to less or more than full employment output. Furthermore, this state can persist. When this occurs, unemployment or inflation results.

The neoclassical synthesis reconciles the unemployment equilibrium of Keynesian theory with the full employment equilibrium of Walrasian theory. This is accomplished in two ways.

In one way, consumption and investment demand are increased if unemployment exists as a result of the impact of price deflation on the deflated money supply and thus interest rates. This Keynesian effect can be limited in its scope because interest rates may not fall and investment may not react to lower interest rates.

In the second way, the function determining consumption is modified so that when wages and prices decline due to unemployment, the purchasing power of some portion of wealth increases. This leads to an increase in consumption at every level of income or employment. As a result, *in principle* consumption plus investment will in time add up to the full employment output. Thus *in principle* the market mechanism will assure that in equilibrium the economy is at full employment. Furthermore, if markets are competitive, this equilibrium will also satisfy Smith's dictum. (An argument symmetrical with that for unemployment is made for inflation.)

The above is the agreed-upon core of the neoclassical synthesis. Policy differences among believers arise from two sources: differences as to the determinants of the volatility of investment, and the extent to which an active monetary or fiscal policy is necessary or effective. We will contrast the policy views of a model New-New Economist (or monetarist) with those of a New Economist (a conventional Keynesian).

For a model New-New Economist, dominant during [the early Nixon era], instability is due to economic policy, especially the inept management of money by the Federal Reserve. Some economists, for example Professor Friedman of Chicago, argue that the foundation of a correct economic policy is stability in the rate of growth of the money supply. Once this is achieved, market forces can be depended upon to yield full employment. If past errors lead to deviations from full employment demand, then the appropriate current policy is to set and sustain the required stable monetary growth. The ways by which money works its "magic" are so complex, subtle, and powerful that attempts to react to current deviations of income or employment from target can only aggravate the situation by either too much stimulus or too much constraint. In other words, the establishment of a stable monetary environment is the best tack for policy. Within such an environment, after any disturbance the system will move toward equilibrium quickly and vigorously. Attempts to speed this process will lead to overshooting the target.

The New Economists, dominant during [the Kennedy–Johnson era], do not have this faith that the economy will settle down into and sustain full employment if left to its own devices. On the whole the New Economists do not offer any cogent explanation of the volatility of private demand: their theory of investment demand leaves little scope for volatility. Nevertheless, they believe that demand—both investment and consumption—varies, so that over any period consumption and investment demand may be greater or smaller than what is necessary for full employment output.

Although there is general agreement among the New Economists that in theory price flexibility will lead to full employment, they also generally hold that this mechanism operates too slowly or that there are serious barriers to wage and price changes. Thus market forces cannot be relied upon to eliminate unemployment or inflation. Active intervention—either by monetary or fiscal policy—is needed to offset the shortfalls (and excesses) of demand. Fiscal policy which operates upon demand directly by government expenditures and indirectly by taxes is the favored policy instrument of the New Economists.

Thus the economic theory of the New and the New-New Economists is identical. Policy differences follow from judgments as to the causes of the volatility of demand and beliefs as to the efficacy of monetary and fiscal measures to offset changes in private demand. Whereas the economists of the Kennedy–Johnson era emphasized the power of fiscal policy, those serving Nixon in their first years in power emphasized the power of monetary policy.

Economic Theory and Economic Performance

Three specific shortcomings of the American economy are due to the biases introduced into policy as a result of the neoclassical synthesis:

(1) The deficiency and decline in the standard of public goods and "public utility" output provided by government and regulated private enterprise, together with an apparent deterioration of contributions to the quality of life from noneconomic institutions.
(2) The unequal and unfair distribution of private income and the gains from economic "growth" and "progress."
(3) The emergence and persistence of inflationary pressures and recessions that are resistant to conventional monetary and fiscal devices, combined with growing evidence that the financial structure is fragile.

The deficiency and decline of public goods and the deterioration of the noneconomic fabric generating social well-being are related to the definitions of well-being used in the theory. The absence of any income distribution policy reflects the neoclassical view that technical production relations determine the distribution of both income and the gains from growth. The persistence of inflation and the growing fragility of the financial system are related to the misinterpretation of the role of finance in the Keynesian framework and the resulting misuse of policy instruments.

The American economists who have had the ears of our recent princes have helped lead the country astray:

(1) By being Walrasian and Paretian in their approach to economic welfare. Commodities are the basic unit in the Paretian analysis of welfare. In this view, households are not embedded in a society that creates and defines wants. As a result of this commodity emphasis, GNP, i.e., the summation of the value of commodities

(and services) produced per capita, is taken to be the measure of social welfare. The limitations of this measure, when want satisfactions are taken as the objective of economic life, are ignored.

(2) By not having a Marxist thrust to their theorizing with respect to saving, investment, and the distribution of income. Standard economic theory is based upon two constructs—the preference system and the production function—which yield saving and investment (and thus growth) as well as the distribution of income. The adviser-economist believing in the validity of the neoclassical synthesis can evade facing up to questions of income distribution and the desired rate and composition of economic growth.

(3) By using a special version of the Keynesian model in a domain where it does not apply. The standard theory appends the "Keynesian" monetary–fiscal analysis to a Walrasian general equilibrium system. The Walrasian system—in spite of complications added by analysts—is essentially a timeless barter paradigm. Keynes treated an intensely financial capitalist economy which normally experiences business cycles. "Fine tuning" of such a capitalist economy cannot be achieved. Capitalism is flawed, in the sense that stability is essentially destabilizing, i.e., a capitalist economy tends to explode once it is stabilized at or near full employment.

If meaningful changes in policy are to take place, it will be necessary for economic analysis to broaden its concept of human wants and goods (become Marshallian), deepen its understanding of income distribution and growth so that the social and the technical determinants are integrated (become Marxist), and widen its view of the possible modes of operation of a capitalist economy and understand the limitations of policy (become Keynesian).

Where the American Economy—and Economists—Went Wrong (1972)

Human Wants and Goals

The theory of choice is introduced into academic economics by postulating that each household has a preference system and an initial allocation of goods. Preference systems are unexplained and unchanging. They might be genetic characteristics, except that in some of the parables that are told it seems as if the preference systems were there at the creation and will last until the final holocaust. Similarly, the initial bundles of goods are unexplained—they presumably are some heterogeneous manna which falls unto each unit. A trading process is defined which is a good-for-good exchange (barter) with recontracting so that no one ever makes a false trade (no errors and no regret are possible). By barter, each unit achieves its best possible commodity set.

The above is the Walras–Pareto view of choice theory. The alternative Marshallian view is very different. In this view, man is a social animal living in family units with wants that can be satisfied in various ways, private commodity flows being only one among many. There is no presumption that the maximization of those satisfactions that flow from wants that marketable commodities and services satisfy is a fit measure of welfare. In particular, private wants can be satisfied by public means.

There is also no presumption that traded commodities when summed at market prices yield the relevant concept of income. A Marshallian perspective leads to a broader concept in which humane treatment and civil behavior yield satisfaction.

The Paretian view that welfare is maximized by exchanges among goods allows no place for free and nonappropriated goods. Thus the deterioration of the quality of air was not considered a major factor in economic analysis until thrust upon the economist by the environmentalist. The paradox that an hour's drive to work tends to increase GNP, whereas a 20-minute walk does not, is evidence that GNP does not in any meaningful sense measure economic welfare.

The neoclassical way of looking at choice induces a bias, so that economists tend to value private consumption out of private disposable income highly and to discount the value of the consumption of public goods. The costs and benefits of alternative social organizations are not examined. The economists who have helped mold policy have not been especially sympathetic to considerations such as Marshall put forth: "The spirit of the age induces a closer attention to the question whether our increasing wealth may not be made to go further than it does in promoting the general wellbeing; and this again compels us to examine how far the exchange value of any element of wealth, whether in collective or individual use, represents accurately the addition which it makes to happiness and wellbeing" (Marshall 1938 [1890], 85).

The output of the public sector is part of GNP and the satisfaction-producing system of an economy. Nevertheless, Professor Tobin described choices made while he was advising Kennedy by remarking that "while we sympathized with the stress which J. K. Galbraith and other liberals placed upon the importance of expanding the public sector, we did not agree that total output and growth of output had ceased to be socially important" (Tobin 1966, 22). Of course, Tobin really knows that a growth of public output is a growth of output; nevertheless, the meaning of his assertion seems to be that resources used to provide parks, public hospitals, public schools, and the safety of persons are resources wasted. Throughout the '60s and into the '70s, aside from the military, the preferred instrument for generating expansion has been a tax cut or loophole, i.e., the shifting of command over resources to private hands.

Even when dissatisfaction with poverty or income distribution is manifest, the neoclassical bias leads to advocating policies such as the Nixon welfare reforms, the McGovern social dividend, or a negative income tax. This is so even though there are strong indications that large-scale improvements in welfare programs will lead to inflation which "inflates out" a large portion or even all of the welfare gain. There is an apparent inability to conceive of poverty as being system caused: all that is needed to correct the lot of the poor is to have the government act as a lady bountiful.

To a neoclassical economist, GNP and employment, not the satisfaction of human wants, are the objectives of national economic policy. Tobin, in his previously cited lecture, relates how Kennedy, bowing to conservative pressures during the campaign, promised a balanced budget. This constraint was evaded, however, when "the Berlin crisis in the summer of 1961 activated one of the escape clauses in the initial balanced budget pledge, leading to a defense buildup of some $3 billion in annual expenditures" (Tobin 1966, 10). This comment makes one wonder whether Vietnam was not of the same cloth as the Berlin crisis: it is good for GNP, whether it is good for the people is not relevant.

This bias introduced by using GNP, which includes military expenditures as an index of welfare and of success for economic policy, shows up in foreign aid as well as in domestic economic policy. Need I recall that as little as four years ago Pakistan was hailed by house intellectuals as a great success of the foreign aid program? Today we know better: the result of our help was the forging of the army that carried out the great massacre of Bengal.

The bias introduced by modern economic theory leads to a neglect of all but GNP as an indicator of aggregate economic welfare. Concern with the shape of GNP is needed as an antidote to the current practice: military expenditures, while using resources, *do not* in general contribute to "welfare" as measured by private and public consumption; other dimensions of public expenditure, such as parks and schools, do. Unless an economic theory makes this distinction it cannot be useful as a guide to redirecting priorities.

The Distribution of Income and of the Benefits of Economic Growth

The neoclassical synthesis leads to a neglect of income distribution as a matter of prime policy concern. In neoclassical economics, at full employment the proportion of GNP going to wages and profits is determined by characteristics of the production function: technique determines relative shares. A well-known proposition in this theory is that if production conforms to a particular relation, a Cobb-Douglas function, as is often assumed, then the shares of wages and profits in GNP are fixed and independent of the proportions of capital and labor used.

If technique determines income distribution, then the lot of the poor and near poor can be improved only if growth of output per person takes place. The iron constraint of techniques implies that a meaningful increase in the proportion of income going to the poor cannot be achieved. This theory will make a man of goodwill an almost devout believer in the virtue of economic growth.

The neglect of the distributional aspects of the saving and investment process was shown by Kennedy's liberal Democratic Council of Economic Advisers. Once again, citing Tobin, their growth orientation disposed the Council and the administration "to favor a policy mixture which would provide for a high proportion of public and private investment in full employment GNP." Thus, policy measures such as "a tax credit for investment and liberalization of depreciation values" were adopted (Tobin 1966, 22–23). In the years 1964, 1965, 1966, and again in 1968 and 1969, these measures, together with the expectational climate, led to an investment boom. The social process that generates more saving results in a shift of income to gross profits.

The investment boom which took off in 1964, together with the war in Vietnam, succeeded in reducing unemployment. This induced a sharp rise in the income of the poor. As a result, starting in the middle 1960s and continuing through 1970, blue-collar factory workers, who had been employed prior to the achievement of tighter labor markets, did not enjoy any increase in their real per capita disposable income. Some of the observed resentment, social disarray, and community disorganization reflects these facts. Over a five-year period, 1965–70, real take-home income of a representative factory worker *declined* by some 2.5 percent; this followed a five-year period, 1960–65, in which a 13.3 percent growth took place.

Simultaneously, this group—the employed lower-middle-income worker—suffered a decline in income received in kind from public goods.

There is an inconsistency between guns and butter once full employment is achieved. Similarly, at full employment there is an inconsistency between investment and consumption. At less than full employment, investment and consumption are complements;

Where the American Economy—and Economists—Went Wrong (1972)

at full employment, investment and consumption are substitutes. Growthmanship tries to raise the rate of growth of full employment GNP by increasing the proportion of investment in income. It will succeed as it raises the proportion of profits in income. A rise in guns along with a rise in investment and a shift of some of the increased wage bill toward previously unemployed workers leads to an inflationary process which tends to reduce the real income of previously employed workers. The attempt by middle-income workers to sustain a level or a trend in consumption reduces household saving ratios. This further aggravates the inflationary tendency.

Furthermore, the combination of private consumption demand, private investment demand, and increased military spending leads to a decline of real resources allocated to providing public consumption goods. The anti–public sector bias of the economist is reinforced by the way in which resources are made available for investment and military spending by an inflationary process in a full employment economy. Public consumption goods diminish in supply.

Given the facts of American political life, we can posit the following: the rich get relatively little of their consumption from public services; the poor almost always get inferior public goods. Once again, it is those in the middle who get a meaningful amount of their consumption through publicly supplied goods and services. A deterioration here hits them hard. Thus the distributional impact of the policies adopted has been slow or no growth in middle-level private real income combined with a sharp deterioration in the quality and quantity of public goods. It is no wonder that Wallace[*] gains a following; that safety in the streets (the most important public good) and the quality of schools—including busing—are such potent political issues.

Recall Johnson's War on Poverty. The main thrust was education and training, which had to start at virtually the cradle. The prekindergarten of Operation Head Start embodies this philosophy. The philosophy of Operation Head Start means that all the poor who missed prekindergarten or other special training are, except for the lucky or the gifted, doomed to a life of poverty; what is called

---

[*] Governor of Alabama George Wallace.

a dead-end life. The Dead-End Kids and the unemployed of the Depression years were such because of system behavior. Their poverty was not their fault. The poor of the liberal's War on Poverty are poor because they are deficient. The liberal's War on Poverty was born out of neoclassical theory in which it is the poor—not the economy—that is to blame for poverty. The War on Poverty tried to change the poor, not the economy.

The negative income tax, which with another label is part of Nixon's (and McGovern's) program, is an admission that the economic system cannot be made to operate so that all who desire to work are able to achieve a socially acceptable standard of life. Work is in itself a want that man strives to satisfy. The conventional neoclassical theory, as it confronts poverty in the midst of plenty, offers a truly dismal solution: the unworthy poor are to be barred from even the satisfactions and social intercourse of work by a perpetual dole.

A further example of the dead end to which neoclassical economic theory leads appears as an exercise on the "Future National Output and the Claims Upon It" in the 1970 *Economic Report of the President* (78–84). This exercise consists of projecting GNP available by taking the 1969 actual GNP of $932.3 billion and multiplying it by $(1.045)^n$ (it is assumed that GNP will grow at 4.5 percent per year), where n is the number of years, from one to six, in the exercise. The projected GNP available in 1975 is $1.2 trillion.

The claims on GNP are obtained by taking the actual division of GNP in 1969 among federal government, state and local government, personal consumption, and gross private investment and multiplying each component by an assumed appropriate growth rate. The first conclusion of the exercise is that "existing claims upon the growing available national output already exhaust the probable output and real national income that the economy can generate for several years to come" (CEA 1970, 83). This is so in spite of the reduction in federal government purchases from $92 billion to $84 billion over the years 1969–75.

This conclusion is reached by ignoring the distribution of income and consumption. Consumption is by far the largest claim on

Where the American Economy—and Economists—Went Wrong (1972)

available GNP. In the president's exercise, consumption rises from $576 billion in 1969 to $769 billion in 1975, a compound growth rate of 5 percent per year. Given that the labor force grows at 1.75 percent per year, this projection assumes a 3.25 percent growth in consumption per labor market participant. The projection assumes it worthwhile to use resources so that the consumption of those in the upper 5 percent of the income distribution grows in excess of 20 percent per labor market participant between 1969 and 1975.

In a country hard pressed for resources it is worth asking whether a proper sense of national priorities is evidenced by a policy which blithely assumes that the national interest is served equally well by increasing the personal consumption standard of the representative upper-income family, say, one now making $40,000 per year, by 20 percent in real terms over a six-year period as by increasing the consumption standard of a poor family, say, one now making $3,000 per year, in the same ratio.

Table 5.1 Personal Consumption (in billions of constant dollars)

		1969	1975 Administration Example	1975 Alternative Example	Assumed Annual Growth* (in percent)
Top	5 percent	115.2	153.8	127.9	(1.75)
Next	75 percent	432.0	576.6	531.5	(3.5)
Bottom	20 percent	28.8	38.6	38.6	(5.0)
Total	100 percent	576.0	769.0	698.0	

Ed. Note: Includes 1.75 percent annual population growth.

Source: CEA (1970)

Let us assume [Table 5.1] that a policy with respect to income distribution that achieves the following contours is feasible: the real private consumption of a representative family in the top 5 percent of the income distribution is not to increase, the real private consumption of a representative family in the next 75 percent of the income distribution will rise at 1.75 percent per year, and the real private consumption of a representative family in the bottom 20 percent of families will rise at 3.25 percent per year. Let us also use the rule of thumb that in 1969 the top 5 percent of the family units had 20 percent of the consumption, the next 75 percent of the family units had 75 percent, and the bottom 20 percent had 5 percent.

The 1975 projected consumption in the president's *Economic Report* is $769 billion. A modest change in national priorities, which reflects the view that it really is not important for the private consumption standards of the representative rich man to increase, that a modest rate of growth of private consumption of the broad middle group is feasible and desirable, and that sustaining the rate of growth of the poor's private consumption is important, will free $71 billion for social consumption. This means that the federal government budget could be well-nigh twice as large in 1975 as projected—or state and local government budgets could be some 50 percent greater than projected.

It is evident that the major potential for reordering national priorities lies in redistributing income and directing the distribution of the benefits of growth. A significant redistribution of income requires a decrease in the share of profits in income. This means that taxes on high incomes from all sources be raised. It also implies that the ratio of private investment to GNP decreases. This in turn means that the productive capacity of the private sectors will not grow as fast as projected. But this does not mean that true capacity does not increase as projected. As we know, the measuring rod of GNP is in itself biased toward giving greater weight to privately produced and used output than to the alternative public use of resources. The public investment made possible by the resources freed from private investment is productive but a safe walk in a park is not, whereas a television program is included in GNP.

Production functions and preference systems are inventions of theorists designed to order and interpret nature. Economic theory based upon these constructs indicates that it is futile to attempt to redistribute income and implicitly therefore to redirect priorities. Alternative varieties of economic theory exist which indicate that income distribution and an economy's priorities are socially

Where the American Economy—and Economists—Went Wrong (1972)

determined. By modifying institutions and usages, both income distribution and economic priorities can be reordered.

The Stability of Full Employment

Correctly interpreted, Keynesian economics is a subtle and complex analysis. Fundamentally, it argues that a financially sophisticated capitalist economy can operate in a number of ways. One is a postcrisis stagnation (the Great Depression of the 1930s), another is slack or small cyclical growth (the Eisenhower era), and a third is an explosive euphoric boom (late Kennedy–Johnson). Although within the theory the proximate determinant of the mode of operation is the amount of investment, the underlying determinants are the speculative portfolio preferences of business firms, households, and financial institutions. Portfolio preferences reflect expectations with regard to the uncertain future. Expectations are determined by the past of the system and views as to the robustness or fragility of business institutions. Thus Keynesian economics is historical in perspective and its propositions are conditional. It embodies the view that in a capitalist framework vital decisions are often speculative.

The fundamental locus of speculative activity lies in the portfolios of households, business firms, and financial institutions. In the Keynesian view, privately owned real capital [comprises] assets in portfolios. Capital holding and expanding the stock of capital (private investing) are speculative activities.

The Keynesian model views the behavior of the economy as being subject to influence and control by policy. Throughout most of the capitalist era, policy has been inadvertent. Economic theory offered no guide—and pre-Keynesian theory was fundamentally incapable of acting as a guide—to policy relating to the dynamic attributes of the economy.

Standard economists of today fall into two camps: those who virtually ignore their economic theory when they give policy advice, and those who give policy advice that is consistent with the neoclassical synthesis. The first group typically are the "liberals" and are often called Keynesian. Their policy advice is heavily dependent upon the policy rules worked out when the Great Depression posed the policy problem. The second group typically are the "conservatives"; sometimes they are called monetarists. Fundamentally, they hold that no policy is the best policy—but cannot agree on what constitutes "no policy." In detail, they argue that there are "natural" rates of unemployment and economic growth and that monetary and fiscal policy should be directed at avoiding the distortions that accompany inflation. Hence monetary stability—not allowing monetary phenomena to rock the boat—is the major contribution that policy can make. Fundamentally, this view is dismal, for it holds that these natural unemployment rates, growth rates, and income distributions are given by "nature," and if they are not satisfactory, it is too bad. Nothing can be done to appreciably affect them.

The interpretation of Keynesian economics advanced here—that Keynesian economics emphasizes the dominance of speculation—is at variance with that given in textbooks.

In particular, the standard device of the neoclassical synthesis, wedding the Keynesian apparatus to a Walrasian output-determining system, is not legitimate. That speculative considerations centering around financial markets can dominate production function characteristics in determining economic system behavior is a fundamental theorem of the Keynesian model. This is foreign to the neoclassical synthesis. The Keynesian view is that a capitalist economy generates a cyclical, dynamical process in which the evolving financial environment determines the system state. The Walrasian view is a "barter" paradigm, where activities which result in steady growth are carried on as if goods were traded for goods. As a result of the way in which the standard Keynesian model has developed, economic policy, when guided by what passes for Keynesian theory, ignores the transitory nature of a particular mode of system behavior.

In the stagnant mode of system behavior, households and firms have recently experienced sizable losses and they view the future with apprehension. The desired liability structure of firms includes little in the way of debt instruments. In fact, the existing liability structure is viewed as being too risky. Symmetrically, households and financial institutions insist upon a great deal of protection in the assets they hold.

Where the American Economy—and Economists—Went Wrong (1972)

As the stagnation continues, fears are attenuated so that stagnant behavior is succeeded by a mode in which some slight adventures in liability structure and asset composition are hazarded. Investment will be accompanied by increases in corporate debts and asset owners' portfolios will hold an increasing proportion of risk assets. In this second stage, the system might exhibit short cycles, [and] monetary policy might very well seem to be effective.

In the third mode of behavior, the economy is euphoric in the sense that long-run expectations are taken to be very favorable. Capital goods, productive capacity, and liability structure are viewed as being too conservative. Simultaneously, asset holders and financial intermediaries are willing to diminish the ratio of money and safe assets in their portfolios.

The transition from the second state of cyclical and slack growth to the third state of euphoric expansion is the point at which the shortcomings of the neoclassical synthesis led to our current malaise. The model for policy which the Kennedy economists took to Washington was a Keynesian depression model. This model often takes the form of a complex econometric model. Upon closer inspection, this presumably sophisticated model is economically naïve; it is no more than an expanded multiplier. It is a depression model in which both consumption and investment (in guns and butter) can be obtained. Neither the complexity of the financial structure nor the subtle interactions between the financial and the real that characterize both the economy and the theory of Keynes are evident in these models.

Given the amount of slack that developed during the Eisenhower years, this model was an adequate guide to policy when Kennedy took office. The tools and techniques that Professor Alvin Hansen had developed at Harvard before World War II for a deeply stagnant economy were for the moment appropriate to the moderately stagnant economy. There was no need to allow for differences between desired and actual balance sheets for households and business firms in making policy decisions.

However, as the expansion was sustained and the slack absorbed, the expectational climate changed. Business developed a seemingly insatiable desire to invest and a well-nigh unlimited capacity to finance investment by adjusting liability structures and eliminating "excess" liquidity in the asset structure. Similarly, households, banks, and other financial institutions became willing to modify their portfolios to accommodate the demand for finance by firms.

One of the articles of faith of the Kennedy economists was that "a steadily growing fully employed economy is both desirable and attainable" (Tobin 1966, 2). Furthermore, this objective could be achieved by manipulating a limited number of monetary and fiscal policy instruments. This view was derived by manipulating models of a stagnant or slowly growing capitalist economy. But, and this is the essential contradiction, success in achieving a growing, fully employed economy will lead to a euphoric, bullish, speculative mode of behavior of the economy.

In the euphoric mode, as long as the fundamentals of capitalist finance are unchanged, monetary and fiscal constraint will not be effective unless expectations are affected. The ruling expectations of the euphoric mode are such that monetary or fiscal constraints will be offset. Such offsets will cease only after expectations are affected. This typically will result from a financial crisis, crash, crunch, or squeeze, which reveals the essential fragility of capitalist financial institutions. Such a change ushers in a stagnant phase—either a deep stagnation of the Great Depression or a more modest stagnation consistent with the large and activist government of today.

The policy difficulties posed by a high-level slack economy with inflationary tendencies are due to a lack of understanding that policy weapons which are sufficient to move an economy from slack to sustained full employment are not sufficient to sustain full employment. The promises made by the New Economists proved to be illusionary: success, once achieved, proved to be transitory. The concentration upon the analysis of how a slack capitalism works left them without an understanding of the dynamics and the appropriate policy for a fully employed economy.

Conclusion

The current dispirited mood of America reflects the failure of both the economy and the dominant economic theory. It is bad enough when the economy does not deliver what is expected, nay, promised. It is even worse when the policy advisers cannot offer a diagnosis and a program to solve the felt shortcomings. Rather than take the economic doldrums seriously, policy advisers offer for the current ills more of the policy that has failed.

In the work of Marshall, Marx, and Keynes there exist ideas that can be welded into a new synthesis—one which recognizes that man, the object of economic life, is not simply a consumer of GNP, that at our present stage of affluence growth and efficiency may have a low priority compared to equity, and that capitalism is flawed because of its financial system. Furthermore, we have to make do with the flawed system because, once controlled, capitalism is more flexible and responsive than the alternatives. Our devotion to capitalism is in spite of its known flaws. However, being flawed, it should be subjected to fundamental reform and continuing control.

The fundamental flaw of capitalism centers around its financial system, which is inherently unstable. The financial system is also the instrument by which the social surplus is appropriated to private business. Because of this, managers of large aggregations of capital are fundamentally public servants and owners of large accumulations of wealth are fundamentally trustees for the public. The civil management and social use of capital aggregations becomes a major thrust of reform. The name of the game of reform will be power and income distribution. But to undertake this adventure we first have to discard the neoclassical synthesis as a guide to public policy. The economics that is in the current generation of text- or principles books will not do.

Sources

CEA (Council of Economic Advisers). 1970. *Economic Report of the President*. Washington, D.C.: Government Printing Office. January.

Keynes, J. M. 1964 [1936]. *The General Theory of Employment, Interest and Money*. New York: Harcourt, Brace.

Marshall, A. 1938 [1890]. *Principles of Economics: An Introductory Volume*. London: MacMillan.

Tobin, J. 1966. "The Intellectual Revolution in U.S. Economic Policy-making." The second Noel Buxton Lecture of the University of Essex, January 18. London: Longmans for the University of Essex.

Chapter 6

The Poverty of Economic Policy* (1975)

The precipitous decline in industrial production that occurred between September of 1974 and March of 1975 was replaced in April and May by a mild decline, followed by a small increase in June. Whether or not the recession has bottomed out is not as significant as the fact that the forces making for a runaway recession have been contained, if not reversed. The likelihood is that the sharp decline will be succeeded by a modest, if not stagnant, recovery. Because of the standoff between Mr. Ford[†] and the Congress, we can expect no meaningful initiatives with respect to the continuing high unemployment this relative stagnation implies. Thus we are in for a period of comparative tranquility in our economy—a sluggish performance and no disruptions from policy initiatives aimed at improving the economy's performance. As there are no immediate issues of decision on which a stand has to be taken, this is a good time to take a look at some fundamental aspects of our economy and of our economic policies.

Even though it is apparent that 1973–75 is not the beginning of a thoroughgoing collapse, such as took place in 1929–33, this relative success should not prevent us from recognizing that the events of the past decade in general, and of the past two years in particular, with its accelerating inflation, disruptive behavior of money and financial markets, and deepest (and longest) recession of the postwar era, have revealed serious flaws in our economy, the poverty of standard economic policy, and a bankruptcy of conventional economic theory.

Our leading authorities, both in government and out, do not know what hit the economy over the past few years. The standard response of the prominent policy-advising economists (both "liberals" who advise Democrats and "conservatives" who advise

---

* Paper presented at the Graduate Institute of Cooperative Leadership, University of Missouri, Columbia, July 14. Paper 426. Hyman P. Minsky Archive, Levy Economics Institute, Annandale-on-Hudson, N.Y.

† US President Gerald Ford.

Republicans) remains consistent with the advice that they gave four, eight, or 12 years ago; though they have lived through much they have learned little. The events of the past several years are not being used by these conventional seers as critical evidence which puts their theory about the behavior of the economy and their views on public policy to a serious test. As what happened during the past several years deviates from the way the economy is supposed to behave if standard economic theory is valid, the evidence from our recent experience casts doubt upon the validity and relevance of standard theory. Incidentally, both the "liberal" and the "conservative" economists base their advice on the same economic theory. We need a fresh approach to an understanding of what makes our economy run which assimilates and is consistent with experience, and a new age of reform. Reforms are needed that will transform our economic structure, in the light of such a better understanding of how our economy works, so that meaningful and realistic policy objectives can be set and achieved.

Economics has been characterized as a dismal science. This is so because an economist recognizes that there are trade-offs, that the economic system operates so that well-intentioned reforms often have side effects, so that the end result of reforms may be worse, not better, than the initial situation, and that resources and productivity limitations constrain what is possible in both the short and the long run. Thus, even though an economist may be passionately devoted to equalitarian social justice objectives, he often must be a naysayer to specific proposals whose objectives he accepts. The professional training of an economist forces him to recognize that subtle connections exist in the way an economy functions which act as barriers against the easy achievement of objectives that are highly desirable and deeply necessary. Economists thus are forced to be skeptics, and the skeptical attitude sits ill in an age where obvious failures indicate that fundamental reforms are needed.

The economist's role in the formulation of policy is to help design economic structures and government policies that move the performance of the economy in the desired direction and contain, even if they do not eliminate, undesirable side effects of policy

The Poverty of Economic Policy (1975)

actions. To be successful, policy will have to be consistent with a deep and critical understanding of how an economy, with institutions such as we have, works; those who see no evil, hear no evil, and speak no evil about our economy are irrelevant to the pressing needs of our time.

The idea that there are trade-offs which are inherent in the way any economy works can be phrased by recognizing that there is no such thing as a free lunch for the economy as a whole; who pays for the lunch and how it is paid for are the critical questions. We cannot use 5 percent to 8 percent of our productive capacity for war, espionage, and space adventures without losing out someplace else; we cannot improve the income at the supermarket of 10 percent to 20 percent of our population without lowering the income at the supermarket of some other segment of the population; we cannot subsidize the construction of urban sprawl without lowering some other dimensions of income. The relative decline of the United States' per capita income, so that Switzerland, Sweden, and Denmark now have higher per capita incomes than the United States, can be laid to the bleeding of our economy by the excesses of defense; the inflation of prices at the supermarket can be laid in part to the food stamp program; and the decline of our central cities has been the result of the way suburban housing and the infrastructures for the suburbs have benefited from subsidies extracted largely from the dwellers in central cities. Looking to the future, the pervasive government subsidies and acquiescence [to] private taxation by utilities—required by the proposals designed to keep energy output growing at its historic rate—means that other dimensions of our living standards will be lower than they otherwise could be. The benefits to the construction workers, contractors, and the energy industries that the proposed national program in energy that emphasizes the subsidization of supply expansion implies will come out of the standard of life and well-being of other groups: more electric energy means less of other outputs. The question about a free lunch is not whether it exists for some, which it can, but how and by whom the tab will be paid.

Even though economists need to put down the heart-warming enthusiasm of both social reformers and the mindless cheerleaders for the status quo, the postwar period has shown some improvement over earlier times. The fact that the economy has not gone through the wringer of a deep depression in the postwar era is evidence that the progress of the discipline, the economic policies legitimatized by the Keynesian revolution, and the reformed structure of the economy that are a legacy of the Roosevelt era combine to ensure that we now avoid the worst that we have experienced in the past. Although economists must remain skeptics, they need not be as dismal as in earlier times. However, this success in avoiding the worst—a great depression—has been achieved at a cost of chronic and accelerating inflation, the continuance of abysmal poverty, dehumanizing policies that offer minimal protection against the worst ravages of poverty, the institutionalization of inefficiency, and what, for want of a better term, can only be called "rip-offs" by the powerful and the affluent.

Economic policy in the past decade has been characterized by a failure of analysis, a substitution of clichés for reasoning, excessive sentimentality, and a blatant disregard for reality. Although political posturing and opportunism have been responsible for a good deal of what ails us—certainly the erratic course of economic policy since the mid-1960s has disrupted the economy and aggravated problems—the roots of our difficulties are deeper than the economic policy excesses that can be attributed to the Vietnam War and the lack of understanding, character, and integrity in policy formation that characterizes the Nixon–Ford years.

Before we get into the details of our argument we have to set some ground rules. We are not interested in the behavior of some idealized economic order—whether the idealization takes the form of a mathematical construction or a fictional idealization. We are interested in the behavior of the economy as it is—with institutions, usages, and government interventions that are the product of history and which embody past errors of analysis and policy. Our policy objective is not the achievement of some abstract perfect order—we are not utopians—but rather, we need to do better than we have. We never want to be caught in the trap where the ideal is the enemy of the good. Furthermore, in doing economic analysis and policy prescriptions we need to recognize that much as we may try we will not be able to solve economic problems once and for all, and that there will be a need to repudiate at a later date what was, when instituted, an apt policy thrust; just as today we need to reform and perhaps reject inherited policy strategies that in their time were apt and desirable.

Fundamentally, a capitalist economy is flawed in three dimensions. Because of its financial system, capitalism tends to generate both speculative booms and deep depressions, i.e., the economy is not stable. The processes of capitalist accumulation tend to generate monopolistic and near-monopolistic market structures together with financial practices and government policies which sustain these monopolies; i.e., the economy is not efficient. In spite of the fact that the aggregate ability to produce increases and that production in our complex modern world is a deeply cooperative affair, private wealth ownership and the effects of monopoly power upon relative wages and profits rates mean that capitalism as we know it leads to the creation, maintenance, and extension of extremes of poverty and wealth; i.e., the economy is not equitable. Thus economic policy, within a capitalist framework, has to be based upon a theory that helps us understand the flaws if we are to overcome or contain the instabilities, inefficiencies, and inequities. To be useful, economic theory has to be critical.

Financial Instability

A fundamental and inescapable flaw of a capitalist economy centers around the tendency of such an economy to generate speculative inflationary booms followed by financial crises, debt deflations, and deep depressions—to generate what occurred in the late 1920s and the early 1930s. This instability exists because investment—which is always a decision to use current resources for a payoff in the often quite distant future—is a speculative activity in all economies.

However, in a modern capitalist economy with a sophisticated, complex, and evolving financial structure, overriding speculative elements exist, which revolve around how investment and ownership of the stock of inherited capital assets is financed. In a capitalist economy liability structures of increasing complexity exist and lead to a wide range of financial assets for portfolios. The debts and thus the cash payment commitments these financial instruments embody reflect past and present views about the future. These views are volatile in their response to successes and failures in the economy. A run of good times increases the desired and acceptable amount of debts, and such increases in debt finance the demand for capital assets and investment, which means even better times, and so on. On the other hand, disappointment in the performance of capital assets as generators of cash leads to the failure of income to support inherited debt structures, which leads to a desire to reduce debt and thus investment, which leads to even greater shortfalls of income, etc. This financial instability is inherent in capitalism, and many accommodations and institutions of a capitalist economy are designed to enable us to live with such instability.

A sophisticated financial system—banks, Wall Street, the various money market institutions—is really the necessary and distinguishing characteristic of an advanced capitalist order. The basic speculative element which is special to a capitalist economy is the extent to which debt is used to finance the construction of new real capital assets as well as for the holding of existing real capital assets. In Table 6.1 some details of the developments of the finances of nonfinancial corporations over the years since 1950 are exhibited. Over this period as a whole a marked increase in the ratio of total corporate debt to the gross internal funds generated by corporations (column II) has taken place. On closer inspection, the development of the debt–cash flow ratio falls into two steps: an early period, 1950–65, in which this ratio showed no perceptible trend (this ratio was lower in 1965 than in 1950), followed by a decade (1965–74) in which the ratio increased from 6.15 to 10.46.

Debts are promises to pay cash as interest and as a repayment of principal. The cash that corporations have available to meet these commitments is the difference between their receipts and the cost of purchased materials, services, and labor: gross internal funds is a good, though not perfect, measure of such available cash. The payments corporations need to make are reflected by their total

Table 6.1 Financial Developments over the Postwar Period: Nonfinancial Corporations, 1950–74

Year	I Ratio of Fixed Investment to Internal Funds	II Ratio of Total Liabilities to Gross Internal Funds	III Ratio of Total Liabilities to Demand Deposits	IV Ratio of Total Liabilities to Protected Assets
1950	1.069	6.91	5.12	2.88
1951	1.070	6.93	5.33	3.03
1952	1.044	6.78	5.40	3.18
1953	1.122	7.02	5.59	3.18
1954	1.00	6.55	5.39	3.25
1955	.905	5.98	5.95	3.362
1956	1.066	6.49	6.47	3.984
1957	1.109	6.45	6.79	4.245
1958	1.002	7.025	6.887	4.256
1959	.929	6.452	7.728	4.216
1960	1.038	6.894	8.666	4.930
1961	.978	7.109	9.137	4.947
1962	.931	6.454	9.646	5.079
1963	.931	6.664	10.333	5.234
1964	.906	6.196	10.945	5.735
1965	.961	6.154	12.044	6.362
1966	1.016	6.272	13.121	7.311
1967	1.043	6.746	13.514	7.757
1968	1.111	7.562	14.405	8.353
1969	1.270	8.542	14.88	9.666
1970	1.319	9.346	15.76	9.909
1971	1.170	8.535	16.60	9.562
1972	1.212	8.457	18.218	10.377
1973	1.283	8.827	20.939	11.961
1974	1.421	10.461	23.038	11.904

Source: Computed from Federal Reserve (1950–74)

liabilities, whether these liabilities are short term or long term, and the interest rate on their liabilities. As is well known, the interest rate on corporate liabilities has increased markedly over the decade 1965–74 and the average term of debt has decreased. Thus the cash payment commitments have increased by an even greater ratio than indicated by the rise in the liability to gross internal funds ratio from 6.15 in 1965 to 10.46 in 1974. This implies that if corporations are to achieve the same ratio of funds available to meet financial commitments to financial commitments in, say, 1975, as ruled in 1964, they may have to double their gross internal funds over the amount achieved in 1974. We hear much about the ratings of corporate bonds and the need for internally generated funds by corporations; what we don't hear is that the debt structure of firms that we now have generates an independent inflationary thrust to the economy. To achieve sufficient internal gross profits to improve the quality of their debts, firms would need a substantially higher dollar markup on their out-of-pocket costs of production than that which ruled in the early 1970s. Profit inflation at a substantial rate is necessary to make corporations as healthy as they were earlier. This need for profit inflation is a lingering effect of earlier inflation-and-investment booms.

In addition to the rise in the ratio of liabilities to cash flows, the period since 1950 has witnessed a marked deterioration in the holdings by corporations of secure assets relative to debts. Thus liabilities were 5.12 times demand deposits in 1950 and 23.04 times demand deposits in 1975 (Table 6.1, column III). A similar deterioration in the ratio of secure assets to liabilities is shown in column IV of Table 6.1, which shows that liabilities relative to protected assets (total bank deposits plus government debt of corporations) has risen from 2.88 in 1950 to 11.9 in 1974. Corporations have been stripped of their liquidity.

One reason for the rise in the ratio of debt to cash flows and secure assets is shown in column I of Table 6.1. The measure of fixed investment divided by internal funds shows us how corporations have financed their additions to capital assets; up until the mid-1960s this ratio showed no perceptible trend, and in many years,

Table 6.2 Financial Developments over the Postwar Period: Commercial Banking, 1950–74

Year	Ratio of Financial Net Worth to Total Liabilities	Ratio of Total Liabilities to Protected Assets	Ratio of Demand Deposits to Total Liabilities	Ratio of Bought Funds to Total Liabilities
1950	.0748	2.88	.6858	.035
1951	.0740	3.03	.6905	.035
1952	.0735	3.18	.6845	.056
1953	.0753	3.18	.6694	.037
1954	.0763	3.25	.6612	.039
1955	.0777	3.362	.6555	.042
1956	.0799	3.984	.6462	.047
1957	.0825	4.245	.6257	.047
1958	.0810	4.256	.6086	.049
1959	.0834	4.216	.6053	.048
1960	.0857	4.930	.5902	.046
1961	.0847	4.947	.5690	.054
1962	.0831	5.079	.5411	.046
1963	.0765	5.234	.5118	.056
1964	.0764	5.735	.4923	.068
1965	.0734	6.362	.4643	.084
1966	.0730	7.311	.4430	.104
1967	.0698	7.757	.4288	.109
1968	.0667	8.353	.4150	.129
1969	.0658	9.666	.4065	.179
1970	.0637	9.909	.3932	.158
1971	.0615	9.562	.3766	.108
1972	.0592	10.377	.3573	.121
1973	.0570	11.961	.3268	.157
1974	.0562	11.904	.2968	—

Source: Computed from Federal Reserve (1950–74)

such as 1961–65, fixed investment by corporations fell short of the flow of gross internal funds. However, in the years 1966–74, this ratio never fell below 1.0 and in many years the ratio was well above

1.0; a marked shift from internal to external financing of investment took place.

What is exhibited in Table 6.1 is the evolution of the financial structure of the corporate sector from an initial robustness to a current fragility. In Table 6.2 the evolution since 1950 of the financial structure of commercial banking is exhibited. Without going into details, all of the measures exhibited—the ratio of financial net worth to total liabilities (column I), total liabilities to protected assets (column II), demand deposits to total liabilities (column III), and bought funds to total liabilities (column IV) indicate that the banking system was much less stable and robust in 1974 than it was in 1950. The data indicate that we should not be surprised at the fact that three banks of over a billion dollars each in total assets failed in 1973–74.

It is hard to believe, but it is true, that the standard economic theory virtually ignores financial phenomena of the kind exhibited in these tables. Monetary and financial relations are peripheral to the explanation of how a capitalist economy functions in the standard economic theory that underlies the standard set of policy prescriptions. In an economy with financial characteristics such as our economy possesses, a financial structure is transformed from being robust to being fragile over a period of prosperous years. At the end of World War II, the financial system, due to the legacy of the Great Depression and war finance, was extraordinarily robust. Twenty years of economic growth and mild business cycles occurred before any serious evidence of financial fragility became apparent. The first postwar sign of serious fragility of the financial structure was the credit crunch of 1966. Another threat of financial trauma occurred in 1970, and we have just experienced a third. These threats of financial crises were aborted by Federal Reserve and government actions. We are still engaged in bailouts and refinancing that reflect the financial tautness of 1973–75. Success in bailing out institutions such as the REITs* and the giant banks, which is what is going on now, will set the stage for a renewal of accelerating inflation.

---

* Real estate investment trusts.

The Poverty of Economic Policy (1975)

Thus we have had three threats of a financial crisis in the past decade, and the third threat was accompanied by a serious recession. The very size of the government sector, combined with Federal Reserve and fiscal policy actions, have in each threat prevented the occurrence of a debt deflation, and so far we have avoided a deep depression and prolonged stagnation. However, it is now clear that the economy does generate cycles, that these cycles reflect inherent tendencies in the system, and that these cycles encompass a threat of deep depressions.

Much follows once a cyclical perspective for the behavior of the economy is adopted. Income distribution becomes a result of the cyclical behavior of the economy and policy actions rather than, as standard theory holds, the result of the purely technical conditions of production. The existence of the monopolies and trade unions can be explained by a desire of economic agents to be protected from the losses that would result from price and wage competition in a cyclical economy. Because the prevention of a serious depression is of such overriding public concern, economic policy and intervention are necessary. Laissez-faire is an impossible concept for a cyclically unstable economy. The issue of government regulation and intervention is not whether they will take place, but what kind of intervention will occur and who will in fact benefit.

Thus, once it is recognized that capitalism is inherently unstable, it follows that we need an activist economic policy to constrain and attenuate the effects of this instability. Once an activist economic policy is accepted, the question of what kind of policies will be adopted and whose interests will be served by the adopted policies becomes important. The discussions of economic policy in the postwar period have faced up to the issue of the use of government policies to prevent serious depressions and some of the inflationary consequences of such policies, but the discussion has virtually ignored questions about how policy affects what kind of output will be produced and for whom output will be produced.

Policy Responses to Recession and Hunger

Because the dominant fact of the past decade—the emergence of financial fragility and thus the recurrent threats of a debt deflation and deep depression—is foreign to the economic theory that acts as a guide to policy, the policy actions of the past several years have been either trivial or inept. Because policy has been guided by irrelevant theory and responded to irrelevant clichés, such as the appeal to the virtues of a nonexistent free enterprise system, or by excessive sentimentality, such as the issue of hunger in America, policy has been inept and often irrelevant to the serious issues we confront.

A most striking aspect of the irrelevance and wrongheadedness of policy has been the recourse to the dole, not only in response to the current recession, but over the longer run. A dole is the handing out of cash or services where nothing is required in exchange for the handout. Although much has been made of welfare, the facts are that what is usually meant by welfare is but a small part of the total of such transfer payments in cash and in kind. When the administration and Congress were confronted with the highest unemployment rates of the postwar period their immediate response was to institutionalize and sustain unemployment by increasing the amount and the duration of unemployment insurance and the handing out of cash tax rebates from the Treasury.

Transfer Payments

A major trend in our economy has been the growth of transfer payments. In Table 6.3 the growth of transfer payments from 1929 through the first quarter of 1975 is detailed. From a trivial proportion of personal disposable income in 1929, transfer payments have grown so that they are 15.6 percent of disposable personal increase in 1975. It is also apparent that the greatest growth in transfer payments has occurred during the Nixon–Ford years. Welfare state transfers grew from $61.6 billion in 1969 to $134.6 billion in 1974. They more than doubled in five years. Welfare state transfer payments are a conservative policy response to a characteristic of our economy: the generation of unemployment [and] economic dependency in the midst of what should be a plenitude of opportunities.

Table 6.3 Transfer Payments and Disposable Personal Income: Selected Years, 1929–74, and Quarterly, 1974Q1–1975Q1

	Disposable Personal Income (in billions of dollars)	Government Transfer Payments to Individuals (in billions of dollars)	Government Transfer Payments as a Percentage of Disposable Personal Income
1929	83.3	0.9	1.1
1933	45.5	1.15	3.3
1941	92.7	2.6	2.8
1950	206.9	14.3	6.9
1960	330.0	26.6	7.6
1961	364.4	30.4	8.3
1963	404.6	33.0	8.2
1969	634.4	61.6	9.7
1970	691.7	75.1	10.9
1971	746.4	89.0	11.9
1972	802.5	98.6	12.3
1973	903.7	113.0	12.5
1974	979.7	134.6	13.7
1974Q1	950.6	123.1	12.9
1974Q2	966.5	130.6	13.5
1974Q3	993.1	138.7	14.0
1974Q4	1,008.8	145.8	14.5
1975Q1	1,017.4	158.7	15.6

Transfer payments consist of much more than welfare. In 1973, the last year for which a detailed breakdown of transfer payments is available, they totaled $113 billion, of which $50.7 billion was Social Security and $9.7 billion was hospital and medical insurance. That which is often characterized as the "welfare mess," Aid to Families with Dependent Children totaled $7.2 billion in 1973, a sizable sum but only about 6.5 percent of the total of transfer payments.

Food Stamps

One sleeper in the transfer payments schemes which is now a substantial sum is the food stamp program. This program is an example of how excessive sentimentality affects policy, and in addition of how a poorly thought-out policy effort that reflects good intentions has undesirable side effects. The food stamp program is a significant factor generating the inflation that has so troubled us in the past several years.

Today in the supermarkets of the nation there are two kinds of money that can be used to purchase food: everyday money and the "funny money" of food stamps. Basic to the food stamp program is the definition someplace in the Department of Agriculture of a "standard economy diet" that is defined as a minimum that everyone presumably should have. The cost of this standard diet for families of different sizes is determined, and the food stamp program is based upon the view that a household should spend no more than 30 percent of a specially defined disposable income; i.e., its actual income minus some quite bizarre deductions. If this computed income is sufficiently low that 30 percent of it will not purchase the standard diet, then sufficient food stamps to purchase the standard diet can be purchased for 30 percent of income.

Currently, the standard diet for a family of four is valued at $162 per month. This means that if the take-home pay of a family of four is $400 a month, this family can purchase $162 of food stamps for $113. With a take-home pay of $350 per month the cost of $162 of food stamps will be $95 per month.[1] Inasmuch as the cost to a family of the standard diet increases with family size, the income which entitles a family to food stamps increases with family size. Thus a family that has six children, with wage and salary income of $10,000 a year—which, after Social Security taxes, income taxes, journey to work, and medical cost deductions that are taken to define income for food stamp purposes, might well come to $700 per month—will be entitled to purchase $278 of food stamps for $207. Inasmuch as a family with three children and the same income will not be entitled to food stamps, we have a children's allowance of 23-plus dollars a month for the incremental children in such larger families. Inasmuch as the income tax deduction for children is worth a minimum of $8.75 per month to a family paying income tax, the total children's allowance for the fourth, fifth, and sixth children of our large family may be in excess of $32 per month. For some families, through food stamps, we have a variant of the negative income tax that proved so disastrous to McGovern* in 1972!

What happens to prices when demand is increased without any commensurate increases in supply? The answer is obvious: prices rise. Now let us integrate this single idea into an analysis of the effects of the food stamp program. In 1970, the value of food purchased for off-premises consumption was about $100 billion and food stamps were $1 billion. Food stamps accounted for about 1 percent of food purchases. In 1973, the last year for which detailed information is available, food purchased by households cost about $125 billion and food stamps accounted for $2.2 billion, approaching 2 percent. Newspaper reports on the food stamp program indicate that the costs are now running at the rate of $5.2 billion a year. We do not have current details of national income to enable us to update food spending. Let us assume it now runs at $170 billion, so food stamps are now 3 percent of such food purchases.

Every time the price of the standard budget increases, the value of food stamps that can be purchased for an unchanging number of real dollars increases and the number of households eligible for food stamps increases, because the maximum eligible income is the cost of the standard diet as related to family size divided by 0.3. Today, large families with incomes well above $10,000 a year as commonly measured are eligible for food stamps. Every rise in the price of food in the standard basket—and remember, food stamps can be used for all foods, not just basic or surplus foods—means that eligible households receive larger amounts and more households are eligible; the rate at which funny money is printed increases even more rapidly than the inflation rate. Some 20 million are now on food stamps, and the estimates are that another 20 million are eligible but are not now receiving food stamps. An explosive inflationary

---

* George McGovern, 1972 US presidential nominee for the Democratic Party.

potential exists in the food stamp program even beyond what has already been achieved.

A rise in the price of food mainly hurts those who are close to the eligibility line although not eligible. The near poor are mainly hurt by such a program that is intended to help the poor. If food costs are an element determining collective bargaining demands, and in many areas an indexing of wages, salaries, and transfer payments is in effect, the repercussion is automatic: a rise in food prices translates into a generalized rise in wages, supply prices, and demand for goods. The beneficiaries of income increases "fight it out" with the food stamp recipients for available food, raising prices another round, which raises both the eligibility level for food stamps and the amount paid out to prior recipients of food stamps, and so on. Food stamps constitute an independent cause of an inflationary spiral.

If ever there was a program in which sentimentality with regard to hunger and clichés about consumer sovereignty dominated analysis and reason it is the food stamp program. There must be a better way than the road we have traveled. I will get back to transfer payments before I finish.

One striking characteristic of policy over the past 40 years has been a consistent thrust toward the generation of income independent of current labor market participation. If an economy is felt to be unable to generate a sufficient number of jobs to employ all who are willing and able to work under one set of social rules, then one way to eliminate unemployment is to change the social rules so that labor market participation is decreased. Raising the school-leaving age and improving retirement benefits [while lowering the eligibility age] is one tack; another is to improve the money income that is available independent of labor market participation. Welfare, unemployment insurance, and food stamps are additional elements in the anti-employment thrust to policy.

No matter how much the process is obscured by artifacts like the Social Security trust funds, transfer payments always involve a transfer of income from those who are active in the labor force to an inactive segment of the population. This transfer takes the form of raising the price level of consumption goods relative to the wages of production workers, adjusted for whatever increases in productivity may occur. There is a limit, determined by increased productivity of labor in the production of consumers' goods, to the increase in transfer payments that is consistent with an improvement in the real income of production workers. Shifts in the labor force away from the production of consumer goods and toward the production of investment goods or sterile government goods such as defense, and increases in the scope and generosity of transfer payments that combine to exceed the limit given by increases in productivity in the production of consumer goods, will lead to price increases, i.e., be inflationary. The standard of life not only of the production workers in consumption goods but of the entire population is lowered by such programs if they are carried beyond the limits given by productivity increases in consumption-goods production.

We have to reverse the thrust of policy of the past 40 years and move toward a system in which labor force attachment is encouraged. But to do that we must make jobs available; any policy strategy which does not take job creation as its first and primary objective is but a continuation of the impoverishing strategy of the past decade.

Income Distribution: Poverty and Impoverishment

Much has been made of economic growth as a solution to problems of poverty, and much of policy has been based upon the importance of investment as the major determinant of the rate of growth. Investment means that current resources are used to produce hoped-for future income. One side effect of this emphasis upon investment is the development of liability structures that contain a large volume of debt. The acceleration of financial instability, discussed earlier, is one result of the emphasis upon growth through investment.

The institutionalization of the emphasis upon investment, by means of investment tax credits, accelerated depreciation, and various proposed absorptions of entrepreneurial risk by the government, are all conducive to instability, and by transferring workers from the production of current output to the production of hoped-for future output, the emphasis upon investment is inflationary.

One major development over the postwar period has been a widening of the spread of relative wages among production workers. Over the past decade a sharp rise has occurred in the relative wages of production workers in contract construction. Inasmuch as workers in contract construction are largely employed in the production of capital assets, this increase is a result of the way in which the emphasis upon growth through investment has strengthened the hand of a particular set of unions, at the expense of other workers and the public in general.

Prior to the 1930s, trade unions in the United States were woefully weak. This was so because union strength and power was related to business cycle stages. During periods of good times and labor shortages, labor succeeded in organizing, and during depressions labor unions were effectively reduced in power, if not destroyed. One aspect of the Great Depression was an enormous, 20 percent decline in prices and a 33 percent decline in wages over the years 1929–33. The financial repercussions of such a fall in prices and wages were that the burden of debt increased enormously, leading to successive waves of bankruptcy, each wave making the Depression worse. It was reasoned that if a floor were set to how far wages could fall, then a cumulative debt deflation could not occur. (It is important to note that the New Deal policies were set before the publication of *The General Theory* by Keynes. The monetary and fiscal thrust toward the control of recessions and great depressions had no intellectual respectability.) Thus, once price-fixing by the National Recovery Administration was ruled out by the Supreme Court, it was felt that strong trade unions were needed as a barrier against wage and price deflation. Hence the development of government support of trade union organization. Similar reasoning underlay the agricultural programs.

However, since World War II the various Keynesian devices to sustain income have been available and respectable, and transfer schemes plus large federal government spending, due mainly to so-called defense, have made the floor to income relatively high. Thus the deep depressions that periodically virtually destroyed trade unions have been removed, and the protections of, and lack of control over, trade union power has remained. This has resulted in not only a strong upward thrust in money wages but also an increase in the dispersion of relative wages since World War II. The coexistence of strong trade unions alongside weak trade unions and unorganized sectors is perhaps the worst of all possible arrangements, especially in a society whose morality approves of or tolerates the exercise of "clout." A regime of universal trade union organization with annual tripartite [participation] (labor, management, and government) is superior to what we have.

In Table 6.4, some details supporting the above assertions with respect to wage movements and wage dispersions are presented.

Over the years 1948–73, the average weekly earnings of production workers in manufacturing rose from $53.12 to $165.24. Over the same quarter of a century the consumer price index (CPI) rose from 72.1 to 133.1; the relative CPI was 1.846. If the price level had remained constant over these 25 years an average wage of only $89.91 would have purchased the same bundle of goods that the $165.24 purchased. Of the $112.12 increase in weekly wages, some $36.79 represents real betterment and $75.33 was an offset to inflation. At the same time, the spread of the distribution of earnings of nonsupervisory workers has sharply increased. In 1948, 42 percent of the workers were in industries that fell in the range of plus or minus 15 percent of the average in all manufacturing, 19 percent were in industries where average earnings were more than 15 percent above the average in all manufacturing, and 39 percent were in industries where earnings were less than 85 percent of the average. In 1969, 23 percent were in industries in the bracket of plus or minus 15 percent of the average, 25 percent were in industries where earnings were more than 15 percent above the average, and 52 percent were in industries where earnings were less than 85 percent of the average in all manufacturing. In 1973, the latest years for which data are available, the range of plus or minus 15 percent of the average included 23 percent of the workers in these categories, 27 percent were in industries where earnings were more than 15 percent above the average, and 54 percent were in industries where earnings were less than 85 percent of the average.

Table 6.4 Relative Weekly Earnings of Production Workers (21 Manufacturing Industries, Mining, Wholesale and Retail Trade, and Finance, Insurance, and Real Estate): Average Weekly Earnings Relative to Average Weekly Earnings in All Manufacturing, 1948, 1953, 1961, 1966, 1969, 1973

Weekly Earnings Relative to the Average Production Worker in Manufacturing	1948	1953	1961	1966	1969	1973
	\multicolumn{6}{c}{Percentage of Workers in Each Relative Income Class}
135.6–145.5	—	—	.52	—	9.36	9.3
125.6–135.5	.74	.66	9.60	14.7	.36	7.75
115.6–125.5	18.40	28.84	14.04	10.54	14.17	5.73
105.6–115.5	9.37	4.27	9.73	9.62	10.16	11.08
95.6–105.5	14.36	11.63	12.63	8.66	8.49	.94
85.6–95.5	18.27	10.39	—	4.07	3.89	11.28
75.6–85.5	11.38	6.82	11.57	13.11	13.51	12.28
65.6–75.5	27.24	10.09	4.81	4.0	3.81	2.78
55.6–65.5	—	27.17	35.07	35.0	36.01	38.71
Number of Workers in Above Distributions (in thousands)	23,616	25,947	24,880	28,953	30,865	32,349
Total Civilian Employment (in thousands)	60,621	63,015	70,459	75,770	80,734	88,714
Percentage of Civilian Employment in Above Distributions	38.9	41.1	35.3	38.2	38.2	36.4
Average Weekly Earnings in Manufacturing (in dollars)	53.12	70.47	92.34	112.34	129.51	165.24
Relative Weekly Earnings in Industry with Highest Relation	1.304	1.282	1.346	1.302	1.402	1.450
Relative Weekly Earnings in Industry with Lowest Relation	.682	.644	.628	.610	.607	.574
Range: Highest Divided by Lowest	1.91	1.99	2.14	2.13	2.30	2.52

If we look at the ranges of relative earnings we note that in 1948 the entire distribution ran from 65 percent to 135 percent of the average, less than 1 percent of the production workers were in an industry with earnings that were more than 25 percent above the average, and 27 percent were in an industry with wages less than 75 percent of the average. In 1973, the range runs from 145.5 percent of the average to 55.6 percent of the average, 17 percent of the workers are in industries with more than 25 percent above the average in weekly wages, and 41 percent are in industries with less than 75 percent of the average. Clearly the range has increased.

Of special interest in the light of our above discussion of investment is the course of average weekly earnings in contract construction. In 1948, weekly wages in contract construction were 120 percent of the average in manufacturing, in 1966 they were at 130 percent of the average, and in 1973 they were 145 percent of the average. Contract construction labor is a major ingredient in the cost of housing and in the plant part of investment. But to validate investment in housing or in plant, the rents or profits have to be large enough to pay the interest and the principal on the debts and equities that are issued to finance this investment. The prices of the products of these investments, whether they be the house rents or utility bills, have to be high enough to meet these financial commitments. The absolute dollar values of future rents and future profits have to be larger relative to today's wages in manufacturing than they were for earlier construction. Dollar markups on operating costs have to rise to validate newly produced capital assets that are used in commodity production. This in itself is an inflationary pressure. Either the other dimensions of the standard of living of the rest of the population have to decline to repay investors for the wages of construction workers or a generalized inflation has to occur which raises the future dollar incomes of other workers to a level that is consistent with the higher costs of construction labor.

As long as we are on an investment kick in national policy, the power of the unions and contractors in construction is not only sustained but increased. They will attempt, and by the record to date succeed, in keeping and increasing their current incomes relative to other money incomes. Thus the inflation is not only not a "one round" phenomenon but is a recurring phenomenon, and furthermore, it is at an accelerating rate.

When in 1948 the average contract construction weekly wage was 120 percent of the average weekly wage in manufacturing, the average worker could more easily pay the rents needed to validate housing costs than when the average wage in contract construction was 145 percent of the average wage in manufacturing, as in 1973. Wage increases have priced new housing out of the average worker's ability to pay. As a result, we need ever-increasing doses of subsidies and an acceleration of inflation to sustain housing production.

Maintenance of housing is more labor-intensive than the construction of new housing. Part of the urban problem can be laid to the rise in the relative wages of labor in construction, which has an even greater impact upon maintenance than upon new construction.

What Can Be Done?

The way in which the economy has functioned over the past 10 years and the likely future of our economy, if we keep along the path we are on, are clearly unsatisfactory. The irrational elements in our economy are pervasive. The current crisis is compounded out of flaws which are inherent in capitalism, and institutional arrangements and policy thrusts which in many instances were adopted to alleviate some of the shortcomings of capitalism. These institutional arrangements and policy thrusts are largely ineffective, and to some extent perverse, because policy has not been based upon a deep realization of the flaws inherent in the economy. To do better we have to design our institutions and operate our policies on the basis of an analysis of the economy which recognizes the imperfect nature of the capitalist order of things.

Thoroughgoing reform will touch on many elements of our economy. The market mechanism is a powerful control and coordinating device if the ruling conditions are appropriate—and the most appropriate ruling condition is the absence of private power and control over markets. Technically, this private power and control is the result of monopoly, but in addition to the power over markets due to monopoly-type arrangements, there is the power that comes from size. In place of an antitrust policy, we need a positive policy with respect to size; a simple slogan to guide action is that "bigness is bad."

Bigness

Of course, what is "big" can become an issue. In banking, the sector of the economy I know best, we can define a bank as being too big if it will not be allowed to fail. In the current situation, this may mean an upper limit to size of any bank of something between $5 billion and $10 billion in total assets. (The $60 billion National City Bank and Bank of America are clearly too big.) In the corporate sector, the limits of acceptable size may be more difficult to define, and the difficult question is, what are the alternatives to allowing organizations that are too big? It is easier to break up the giant banks than some of the giant corporations.

One way of looking at the issue of appropriate size and organization is to inquire whether a firm or an industry is going to fully face the test of the market or whether it is going to be protected by various government actions if unfavorable developments occur. Furthermore, we may inquire as to how the prices of what it sells are determined. Is there an impersonal market which determines price, so the unit takes what it can get, or are the prices of what it sells determined by its own or by some regulatory procedure; i.e., it gets what it can take? Many prices, such as utility rates, which by their very nature do not directly reflect current costs, can be best viewed as the result of private taxing power. AT&T, Union Electric, and TWA* are more like tax farmers than the competitive businessman of the economics textbooks.

Where an organization is in the nature of a private taxing authority, an arbitrariness in the prices of outputs is inevitable. This arbitrariness implies an ability by the organization to cross-subsidize: to get revenue from sector A rather than from sector B. But once the issue of cross-subsidization through the taxes of a rate structure is

---
* Trans World Airlines.

admitted to exist, the question needs to be raised whether an entire industry, like the railroads, should meet its costs through taxes in the form of prices, or perhaps part of the costs can be met by taxes on other outputs, or from general revenues. For example, if railways are less polluting and less energy-intensive than trucks, buses, automobiles, or airplanes, it might make sense to add into the fares or cost structure of trucks, buses, automobiles, and airlines funds to subsidize railroads. Special gasoline taxes to subsidize mass transportation are a rational possibility for cross-subsidization. Given the arbitrary nature of particular prices for particular outputs of such capital-intensive, joint-product organizations as railways and automobiles, the possibility exists that relative prices should be used to guide use patterns. In fact, prices for the private taxing and publicly subsidized sectors of the economy are as much a political decision as the income tax schedule.

It is clear that utilities, transportation, and much of communications can be called private enterprise sectors only by an unwarranted extension of the term. We have to escape from the hang-up about nationalization and go back, not to square zero, but to the early 1930s, when we were innovative in creating various not-private and not-centralized public forms of organization that would be authorized to use the private taxing powers not for profits but to serve a publicly defined purpose. If Congress would not be remiss in its oversight functions, if legislatures and boards of aldermen really oversaw such public bodies, I would trust decentralized public enterprise with many tax powers, rather than giant private corporations which stand revealed as corrupt and corrupting institutions.

Construction Wages

It was pointed out earlier that wages in construction have risen relative to wages in other industries. Over the period in which this took place a large part of construction was on government contract—roads, military, space, public housing—and another large part of construction was for the private taxing authorities, such as utilities, communications, etc., which pass on increased costs in their private taxes. In addition, housing construction receives pervasive subsidies through mortgages, etc. Look at the to-do that takes place whenever housing starts fall below some target. Furthermore, business investment, which is heavily construction, is subsidized and encouraged by government programs such as investment tax credits.

Much of construction labor is thus either paid for by government or is protected from market forces by government policies. But if the government pays or protects, should not the government be involved in the setting of contract terms? A general principle should rule government intervention in markets for labor: if the government is to pay, or if private taxes are to pay, then the government should participate in the setting of wages and prices. Thus permanent institutionalized wage and price controls in the construction, utility, health, and defense supply sectors are called for. In construction, I suggest the thrust of government controls should be to roll back wages to the neighborhood of 125 percent of the average in all manufacturing from the present (or 1973) 145 percent of the average.

Reform of Transfer Payments

The transfer payment mess cannot be handled by piecemeal changes. Thoroughgoing reform, based upon an understanding of how our economy works and principles consistent with human dignity and independence, is needed. The principles that should underlie the reform are an affirmation of both the dignity of labor and the social value of receiving income as a right because it is earned. Thus, thoroughgoing reform requires the manipulation of the economy so that there are jobs for all—the young, able-bodied adults, the handicapped, and the aged. Very few should be excluded by principle from the dignity which comes from a realization of their worth through doing a job. The task of job creation is to take people as they are and to generate jobs that fit. No more demeaning the worth of the unskilled by calling their jobs "dead-end" jobs.

In order to have more jobs than workers and not create a strong inflationary thrust, the job guaranteed will have to be at the statutory minimum wage for adults, with some minor differentials for youth. Furthermore, because it is highly desirable that the old, the young, the infirm, and those with child-care responsibilities have the opportunity to work, the jobs that are created should include part-time as well as full-time jobs.

As only the government can take people as they are and fit jobs to them, I propose the creation of an open-ended modern equivalent of the Works Progress Administration (WPA) of the 1930s. As I conceive it, this modern WPA would differ from the public service employment schemes that are being advanced in that the jobs would be at a wide variety of public and semiprivate contracting agencies. The objectives of the contracting agency would be spelled out and the tasks to be performed would be agreed upon. As I visualize this scheme, it guarantees every participant who fulfills job responsibilities an income of $4,200 a year (the current minimum wage rate). By allowing multiple earners in a family, family income can exceed the $4,200 by a margin. There should be no means test for these jobs. Anyone willing and able to work will be put on the projects.

The guarantee of an income through a job is the first step toward the elimination of the welfare mess.

Job creation through the WPA is a completely different strategy from that which has been followed during both Kennedy–Johnson and the Nixon–Ford eras. Whenever over the past 15 years there has been a lack of jobs the policy strategy has been either to reduce taxes—almost always for the already affluent—or to expand government spending on projects that tend to hire the already well-paid workers: defense, space, highways, fancy metro systems, housing, etc. The strategy has been to reduce taxes and increase spending for the already affluent, in the vague hope that some benefit will trickle down to the poor and low-income population. The strategy proposed here is to create jobs at a modest income for all. The immediate benefits are to the unemployed and the low-income population. The already affluent need no breaks, and they can, so to speak, take care of themselves.

In addition to the open-ended WPA, I would immediately resurrect the Civilian Conservation Corps (CCC) of the 1930s. This could, and should, be done independently of the other parts of the scheme. I would make the enlistment period for CCC one year;

The Poverty of Economic Policy (1975)

I would initially program the operation for 1,000,000 young men and women at the ages of 16 through 21. As I see it, the program would involve camp living, the young worker would receive room and board and perhaps $5 a week pocket money, and at the end of the year's participation a lump-sum payment of $2,000 would be made (alternatively, $20 a week could be sent home and a $1,000 lump-sum payment could be provided). I would use military personnel in supervisory functions at the camps. The contracting agency for the tasks would provide the on-the-job supervision. I visualize both urban and rural projects for the corps.

The putting to useful work of such youths will do much to alleviate the social problems of our urban areas. If 40,000 young men and women who do not want to be in school and who are unemployed with no immediate job prospects were removed from the New York City school system and streets, the task for the schools and the public order authorities would be eased. After a year in the corps the young men and women would have broader visions, job experience, and confidence in their capabilities, as well as a stake for either schooling or a start on another job. To my mind it is a criminal neglect of public responsibility that the CCC went off to World War II and never returned. It is of great urgency that it be reestablished as soon as possible.

A third weapon in the arsenal of a job strategy against poverty is the resurrection of the National Youth Administration (NYA) of the Depression days. NYA was a program that provided jobs through high schools and colleges. I would make NYA jobs available to all who want to work, with the high schools and colleges as the contracting agent. Not only would such jobs provide income and work experience for students, if properly run the work performed would remove some of the cost burdens on the schools. NYA should also provide open-ended summer employment opportunities for youths. The object would be to make about $800 per year in income through jobs available to youngsters in high school, half during the school year and half in the summer. I would have the program provide $1,600 per year for college students, again half during the school year and half during summer.

A fourth tool in the program is a universal children's allowance. Because I envisage that the NYA and CCC will pick up the tab for youth income at the age of 16, this program will cover all children until their 16th birthday. At $40 per month, with 61.3 million children under 16 (1972), the gross payment would be $29.4 billion. Eliminating the $750 per child allowance in the income tax would recapture about $9 billion. In 1972, aid to dependent children cost $7 billion, and the elimination of food stamps for children should recapture several additional billions of dollars. Thus the net costs of a children's allowance would be about $11 billion, and doubtless other transfer payment schemes could also be reduced at the same time. Although $11 billion may seem like a great deal, we must recall that total transfer payments were running at almost $160 billion in the first quarter of 1975.

Social Security is another transfer payment scheme that has to be brought under control. Basically, I would eliminate the 62 optional and the 65 "mandatory" retirement ages. I would also eliminate the ceiling on earned income. I would give each person the option of beginning to receive Social Security benefits at the age of 65 or to delay receiving benefits until later, allowing the death benefit and the retirement income to increase on an actuarially sound basis with the age of actual retirement. Such a combination of a right to work (including full or half-time on the WPA) and the ability to schedule Social Security benefits to conform to the wishes and needs of the retiree should enable us to end the pressure for ever-escalating benefits.

What such a program of, say, 2.5 million on WPA ($10 billion), one million on CCC ($4 billion), and some million high school youths and half a million college students on NYA ($1.6 billion) should do is break the back of dependency and poverty, especially if combined with an $11 billion dollar net cost children's allowance. Twenty-seven billion dollars or so seems like a lot, but it is quite manageable in light of our current $158.7 billion of transfer payments. In addition, the workers in WPA, CCC, and NYA will be contributing to national income and well-being through their projects. From the present schemes we get little or nothing.

Furthermore, the WPA approach is a substitute, not an add-on, for two programs adopted during this recession: the extended unemployment insurance, which is blatantly inflationary, and the tax reductions/investment tax credits, which are a continuation of giving to the well-to-do in the hope that something may accrue to the poor. Thus the net costs of a program such as I envisage will be substantially less than the gross costs of the program. It is fiscally manageable.

A vital attribute of the above schemes is that they set floors to income. They do not promise affluence; they promise a reasonable minimum and the dignity of self-reliance. A job-based, rather than a transfer-based, strategy against poverty is a first and vital step toward making our economy work better.

Capital Shortage

A major attempt is under way by the administration, bankers, and Wall Street operators to create a belief that the American economy is suffering from a capital shortage. In particular, they are adding up guesses as to capital needs for the decades ahead and estimating the availability of savings flows in order to come up with gaps of greater or smaller magnitudes that they label as a capital shortage. Their policy proposals are aimed at increasing the flow of savings by tax changes which benefit corporations: larger and permanent investment tax credits, exempting dividend payments from the corporate income tax, increasing the tax-exempt dividend allowance for households, and various schemes of government underwriting of corporate debt, especially in the energy-related fields.

Some of the proposals for government risk absorption for large-scale enterprises could serve as a definition by example of socialism for the rich. Any guarantee against losses due to an inept choice of technology, which is a feature of the proposals for the privatization of the front end of the nuclear energy chain, is a government underwriting of inefficiencies in the choice of techniques.

However, I really want to deal with some more fundamental aspects of the so-called "capital shortage." First of all, it is economic nonsense to speak of a "capital shortage" independent of the price that has to be paid for providing capital on the lavish scale that is proposed. What are we going to give up if we go ahead and build capital assets at the scale envisioned? What are the alternative technical choices which are available which have been rejected in determining capital needs?

We know we have large-scale unemployment and we also know that even at the cyclical peaks our unemployment rates are significantly greater than those of the successful Western European economies. We really suffer from chronic labor surpluses—that is the reason why we need to introduce a permanent WPA, CCC, and NYA into our policy strategy. We have carried substitution against labor too far in much of our technology, and the proposals now emanating from the administration and Wall Street really want to further this tendency.

Central to the argument that there is a capital shortage is the energy crisis. The attempt to meet a presumed need for energy requires enormous sacrifices of current output. We know that Sweden has a higher per capita GNP than the United States. We also know that the energy consumption per capita in the United States is twice that of Sweden. This is a counterexample to the argument that we need more energy to raise our standard of living. If we were as energy efficient as Sweden, we could presumably achieve our current [standard of living] with half our energy consumption. We would presumably be in a position to be a net exporter of oil if we achieved this. Think of what such energy efficiency in the United States would do to OPEC!

But to achieve such energy efficiency we would need to do much more than increase the energy efficiency of the automobiles we use to levels comparable to those achieved in Europe and Asia. We would need to restructure our transportation system—rebuild our railways—and more importantly compact our urban centers so that the journey to work is decreased.

We need to think hard about the social prerequisites for achieving a compacting of our urban centers so that the journeys to work and the journeys to the activities of life are decreased and much less energy dependent. After all, the cheapest, least polluting, and perhaps most healthful way to get from one place to another is either to walk or to bicycle. In our urban centers we should endeavor to arrange things so that for most people the journey to work, to leisure activities, to schools, and to shops is either less than a mile or can be accomplished readily by public transport.

We need to manage our cities and our productive facilities better. We really do not need more of what the capital-shortage people are trying to sell.

I mentioned earlier that bigness is bad because it conveys power. We need to seek alternatives to the giant corporations as the centerpiece of our economic life. Certainly the aberration of corporate structure, which leads to the conglomeration of many types of activities under one corporate umbrella, does much more harm than good. The glamor is gone from the fairy tale about the efficiency of large-scale organization. We now know that the giant corporations and conglomerates are not paradigms of virtue, of efficiency, or of foresight.

What we need is an age of experimentation with alternatives to the giant firms and capital-intensive production techniques. We need a revitalized cooperative movement which looks toward the establishment of cooperatives of various kinds. As overhead wage scales and prices rise in the corporate sectors of the economy, room is made for high and fulfilling standards of living through craft and handicraft production. We really should have a National Handicraft Extension Service, an urban equivalent to the Agricultural Extension Service, which aims at the promotion of localized labor-intensive production: we need craft alliances, furniture craftsmen cooperatives, sewing associations, neighborhood maintenance organizations, and urban cooperative stores. We need experimentation in industrial organization which allows for state, local, and regional ownership. The thrust that developed after World War II, in which the giant corporation was the focus for development and progress, was largely an error and certainly has now run out of steam. Even perceptive Wall Street operators are now calling for massive government subsidization of giant firms. Before we go along that route, we should explore alternatives.

Capitalism's virtues and strengths depend upon the innovations and initiative that come from entrepreneurial involvement not only in management but in the financing of operations. The corruption revealed by Watergate and the bribery of foreign operations may be just the tip of the iceberg. If the "management" of a corporation owns but little of the corporation, if they have learned how to launder money to bribe foreign officials and to pay the levies of CREEP and other politicians, is it too much to suspect that the same techniques can be used to convey bank and corporate funds for the benefit of management? Integrity and the giant corporate organizations as they now exist seem to be mutually exclusive.

Thus what we have is in many ways the antithesis of free enterprise. Only by thoroughgoing reforms, designed not to aid the rich and affluent but to abet the lot of the poor directly—not by trickle-down techniques—can we do better.

The crucial need is for a good hard look at where we are—and what is wrong with where we are. I have offered some suggestions along those lines, and some rather modest proposals for reform of our approach to economic policy.

Note

1. The numbers are from a food stamp program table which rounds out the 30 percent of income standard expenditures.

Source

Federal Reserve Board of Governors. 1950–74. "Flow of Funds Accounts of the United States." Various releases. Washington, D.C.

Chapter 7

Full Employment and Economic Growth as an Objective of Economic Policy
Some Thoughts on the Limits of Capitalism * (1994)

1. Resonance between 1933 and 1993

I participated in a conference on "Financing Prosperity in the 21st Century" at my home base, the Jerome Levy Economics Institute of Bard College, on March 4–6, 1993.[1] March 4 was the 60th anniversary of the inauguration of Franklin D. Roosevelt as president of the United States. The climactic event of the great collapse of American capitalism was the bank holiday that immediately followed the inauguration: officially the bank holiday began on March 6, 1933. Our conference bridged the 60th anniversaries of the inauguration and the bank holiday. The combination of the dating and the topic of our conference made me think of the differences and the similarities between the scenes as Roosevelt was inaugurated and as Clinton was starting his term.

In what follows I argue that the problems President Roosevelt faced 60 years ago and the problems that now confront President Clinton resonate. Each inherited a rich but failed economy. In the situation Roosevelt confronted the failure was so great that almost all agreed that something quite dreadful was wrong, although there was no consensus on what the problem was, why it took place when it did, and how to resolve the problem.[2]

To date, in the 1980s and 1990s, the American economy and the rich capitalist world have dodged the bullet of a debt deflation and a deep depression, such as took place in 1929–33.[3,4] The wholesale bankruptcies, massive asset price deflation, collapse of GNP, and large-scale unemployment, which, if they occur, would create a consensus about the need for drastic government action, have not taken place as yet, and they may not. Whereas in 1933 the economic

---

* Reprinted with permission from P. Davidson and J. A. Kregel, eds., *Employment, Growth and Finance: Economic Reality and Economic Growth* (Cheltenham, UK, and Northampton, Mass.: Edward Elgar, 1994), 149–67.

environment substituted for the gallows in concentrating the collective "mind," the amorphous fear that the current situation breeds has not concentrated that collective "mind."

S. Jay and David Levy, my colleagues at the Jerome Levy Economics Institute[*], diagnose the current situation as a contained depression. Such a depression does not send strong signals that something is seriously wrong with the economy (Levy and Levy 1992). Because of the ambivalent nature of the signals that a contained depression sends, President Clinton's call for change is not well focused. President Clinton and many in his administration may know that something is wrong, but they seem unable to put their finger on what it is.

One thing that is seriously wrong with today's United States economy is that we refuse to accept how rich and potentially productive the economy is. Because we think ourselves poor we are unwilling to use government spending to

(a) first achieve and then sustain a close approximation to full employment; and
(b) create resources which enhance the productive capacity of the economy.

This inhibition against using fiscal powers is due to a combination of unwillingness to acknowledge that we are in fact rich and an unnatural fear of inflation.

What is true for the United States is also true for the other rich economies: they plead poverty and cite the potential for inflation as an excuse for tolerating unemployment.[5]

One way in which the current era resonates with that of the 1930s is that the economies are not living up to the standards that were achieved in the recent past: furthermore, rather simple-minded policy interventions that were fairly successful in the recent past are no longer as effective as they were. This attenuation of the effectiveness of policy interventions indicates that the institutional structure has evolved so that the current economy is not a simple replication of recent economies. An implication of the decline in the efficacy of

---

[*] Name changed to Levy Economics Institute of Bard College in 2001.

Full Employment and Economic Growth as an Objective of Economic Policy: Some Thoughts on the Limits of Capitalism (1994)

policy interventions is that to achieve full employment once again, resource-creation economic institutions need to be changed.

2. The New Model Capitalism of the 1930s

Between 1933 and 1938, by a process of trial and error, the Roosevelt administration responded to the failure of the virtually laissez-faire capitalism of the first third of the twentieth century by creating an interventionist capitalism characterized by a thoroughly revised financial system, a greatly expanded government, and increased regulation of the labor and product markets. The reconstructed financial system aimed to constrain speculation and induce a focus on resource creation. Government spending increased the ratio of utilized to available labor and financed resource creation. The regulation of labor and industry aimed to improve the distribution of income and contain private oligopoly power.[6]

The financial reforms of the 1930s reflected the view that the function of the financial structure was to abet enterprise, not to fuel speculation. Compartmentalization and transparency were the principles that guided financial reforms.

Compartmentalization involved the creation of special financing agencies for different economic sectors (housing, rural electrification, agriculture, and general business are some examples) as well as restricting the liabilities that these different classes of institutions were permitted to issue.

Transparency established the principle that information about the income and activities of publicly held corporations and transactions on the exchanges of the equity and debt instruments of such companies were to be both truthful and widely available.

Transfer payment schemes were not the main thrust of the New Deal.[7] The welfare state, which substituted transfer payments for income from work and owned property, mainly developed after the 1960s, when the measured unemployment rate began its upward trend.

Direct government employment, offered by project-related job programs such as [the] Works Progress Administration (WPA), National Youth Administration (NYA), and Civilian Conservative

Corps (CCC), and large-scale public works projects which funded employment by contractors, were the main government income-providing operations in the 1930s. Able-bodied men and women, as well as youths, obtained income in exchange for work. It became a responsibility of government to provide opportunities for work when the private economy faltered.[8]

Roosevelt inherited a failed and discredited capitalism. A new model capitalism, with an extended set of government interventions in the economy, was put in place. This did not happen in the first 100 days, during which the immediate problems of the acute crisis were tackled. The new model was mainly put in place in the second half of the first term and the first part of the second term (1935–38). The new model, as augmented by the postwar transfer payments of the "welfare state," served the United States well for almost half a century.[9]

3. The Deteriorating Performance

The performance of contemporary capitalisms [has] deteriorated; they have not broken down. Over the past dozen or so years, the new model of 1933–37 has developed ailments that are due to a combination of age and the infusion of laissez-faire adulterants into the institutional structure during the decade in which conservative ideologues administered the interventionist economy. An overhaul of capitalism is needed if the low levels of unemployment, the relative price stability, and the readily observed improvement in the standards of living that characterized the first 20 or so years after the Second World War are once again to characterize capitalist economies.

The pratfalls and comedy acts of the first four months of the Clinton administration make it seem far-fetched to propose that its historic task is to put in place a new model capitalism which would develop programs and institutions which contribute to the creation of human, physical, and knowledge resources, and to their full utilization (full employment). The Clinton administration needs to focus on policies to achieve full employment and to create resources. It needs to keep the programs simple: the New Deal work projects

Full Employment and Economic Growth as an Objective of Economic Policy: Some Thoughts on the Limits of Capitalism (1994)

which were orientated to the achievement of concrete objectives are models for program initiatives.

4. A Bit of History

The usual characterization of the 1933 bank holiday is that "Roosevelt closed the banks." This is not true. By Saturday, March 4, 1933, the day Roosevelt was inaugurated, the governors of some 30 states had closed the banks in their states. Even as Roosevelt was being inaugurated he was informed that the New York banks would not open on Monday, March 6. The bank holiday was a preemptive strike—it moved the resolution of the problem of illiquid and insolvent banks and other financial institutions from the financial community to the federal government.

The United States bank holiday was the climactic event of a great contraction of the American economy that began in October 1929 and lasted until March 1933—some 42 months of well-nigh monotonic decline. The decline was both long and deep. In the United States—and the United States was by no means the worst case—output fell by about 33 percent, prices fell by about 33 percent, and the indices of stock prices (the Dow Jones and the Standard & Poor's) fell by some 85 percent.[10] In the winter of 1932–33, unemployment affected at least 25 percent of the labor force: this in a country where one-third of the labor force was in agriculture.

Sixty years ago capitalism was a failed economic order. Today, as the countries of the Soviet bloc, including the successor states to the Soviet Union, rush to become capitalist market economies, we must not allow the failure of Soviet communism to blind us to the weaknesses of capitalism. We need to examine:

(a) What attenuated the success of the early postwar capitalism?
(b) Why are the capitalist states now in crisis?
(c) What are the contours of a "new" new model capitalism?

The successful capitalisms of the 1950s and 1960s were not the same as the failed capitalisms of the 1930s. In essence, the

1930s system was a small-government, gold-standard-constrained, and essentially laissez-faire capitalism. It was replaced by a big-government, flexible-central-bank, and interventionist capitalism. As Michal Kalecki and Jerome Levy pointed out, a government deficit is the equivalent of investment for maintaining the profits of enterprise.[11] The big-government capitalisms that were put in place in response to the great collapse of 1929–33 protect the economy from a severe fall in aggregate profits, such as occurred in the great contraction of 1929–33. This makes the collapse of asset values, which was so critical to the development of the Great Depression, impossible.

The Roosevelt government used a variety of inadequately funded government employment devices to offset the weakness of the private demand for labor. Even though government deficit financing had a positive effect on profits in the mid-1930s, the scale was too small to lift profits to a high enough level to trigger a resumption of private investment. Government spending sufficient to set off the flows of funds that would lead to a recovery of private investment was not achieved until the massive government defense procurement of the late 1930s.

Full expansion from the Great Depression depended upon the recovery of private investment. This required a new financial structure, learning how that financial structure operated, and a regaining of confidence by borrowers and lenders.

Financial reform was an integral part of the new model capitalism that was set in place in the 1930s.

5. Reconstituting the Financial Structure in the 1930s

During the Roosevelt years, the reconstitution of the financial structure was a major policy task and a great deal of argumentation and negotiation took place before the legislation was adopted.[12] It was not until after 1936 that the new financial structure was in place. It was based upon two principles: compartmentalization and transparency.

The financial structure was reconstituted with special financial organizations for specified functions: for housing, for agriculture, for imports and exports, for commercial banking, for investment

Full Employment and Economic Growth as an Objective of Economic Policy: Some Thoughts on the Limits of Capitalism (1994)

banking, and for deposit insurance. The operations of the publicly traded corporations and the markets in which the trading took place were to be transparent. In addition, the Federal Reserve was reorganized so that the gold standard rules of central bank behavior no longer forced it to be deflationary when prices were dropping drastically and unemployment was high. A government investment bank, the Reconstruction Finance Corporation, was part of the control and support mechanism for the financial structure and for the financing of resource creation: it operated by infusing government equity into transportation, industry, and finance.[13]

The financial institutions of the post-1936 era differed markedly from that which broke down between 1929 and 1933. Once in place, this system of 1936 evolved as a consequence of the profit-seeking efforts of the various institutions. Any institutional structure which sets limits to the self-seeking behavior of economic units will set off reactions designed to evade or avoid those limits. In addition, technological changes impinge upon the profit potential of units in the financial structure in a variety of ways. As a result of institutional and usage responses to constraints and technological changes, the effect upon the operations of an economy of a particular legislated and administered regime will change. Even though the formal Roosevelt financial structure has largely remained in place since the 1930s, the operating details of the structure—as well as the consequences of the structure for the financing of "the capital development of the economy," the portfolios of households, and the stability of the economy—have changed.

As households, firms, government units, and financial institutions learn how a new legislated financial system works, they modify their behavior so that they can best profit within this new structure. In 50 years such changes have led firms to use proportionally less internal finance and new equity issues, and more debt for the financing of investment, even as financial market changes facilitated the greater use of debt to hold positions in existing assets. Over the same time frame, financial institutions changed their portfolios so that private default-possible debt weighed more heavily in the structure of assets, and a general shortening of debt relative to assets took place.

As a result a once-robust financial system became increasingly fragile: fragility implies an increased likelihood that a small stimulus will lead to large changes. A fragile financial structure leads to an economy that is unstable; that is, more vulnerable to a debt deflation.

No serious threat of a financial crisis occurred between the end of the Second World War and 1968. In 1968, the repercussions in the commercial paper market [from] the default of the Penn Central Railroad on its commercial paper rudely awakened the complacent Federal Reserve Board of Governors to remember its responsibilities for maintaining the stability of the financial system. Since 1968 the Federal Reserve has been forced on more than one occasion to take steps to abort what it deems to be an embryonic financial crisis arising from a lack of liquidity of some set of institutions or markets.

The big-government capitalisms of the 1950s and 1960s succeeded in moderating business cycles because the deficits that big governments ran when income turned down sustained business profits when investment lagged. One significant result of the short and shallow recessions of the 1950s and 1960s was that the market power of unions and large oligopolist firms was strengthened. The strong trade unions, the lack of sustained unemployment, and transfer payments abetted the improvement of the lot of those near the bottom of the income distribution.

Inflationary pressures resulted from the combination of higher unit labor costs and the market power of firms.

President Kennedy caught the flavor of the experience of the first two decades after the Second World War in the aphorism "A rising tide lifts all boats." This aphorism has been negated by the experience of [the] 1980s, when the lot of those at the bottom stagnated or deteriorated even though aggregate income measures indicated continued improvement. It seems clear that capitalisms can function in a variety of different ways and that preference systems and the technical conditions of production do not lead to a "law of distribution."

If capitalisms are to be successful in the 21st century they are likely to be different from the models with which we are familiar.

Full Employment and Economic Growth as an Objective of Economic Policy: Some Thoughts on the Limits of Capitalism (1994)

The new model of Roosevelt showed that Kennedy's aphorism can be true. As a result, the ends that a successful economy needs to achieve include a wider distribution of the fruits of prosperity than was achieved over extended periods of time by the pre-1930s model capitalism.

6. Why Are the Capitalist Economies Now in Crisis?

Reagan and Thatcher tried to overthrow the big-government interventionist capitalisms that they inherited. In the United States the major substantive economic changes of the Reagan years were:

(a) the destruction of the revenue system;
(b) the emergence of an economy that was structurally dependent upon the government's deficit financing of a budget that was mainly devoted to transfer payments (including interest on the government's debt) and military spending;
(c) a high-consumption economy due to the increases in the inequality of income distribution and in entitlements;
(d) the fall in the real wage of a large portion of the labor force;
(e) a fragile financial system; and
(f) a rising tide of un- and underemployment.

After a spurious prosperity, largely based upon

(a) an unproductive government deficit,
(b) an enormous expansion of the financial services industry, and
(c) financing schemes that left the country with an excess supply of office structures, highly indebted firms, and nonperforming assets,

the economy of the United States has virtually stagnated for some five years. Furthermore, government spending became even more inefficient as an instrument to create resources, because the high interest rates that were a long-lasting legacy of the experiment in practical monetarism of the Volcker era and the great expansion of the government debt resulted in a huge item in the budget called "interest on the debt."

The Reagan–Thatcher–Bush experience is a second failure of the laissez-faire model. It showed that the laissez-faire model of capitalism cannot meet the performance standards established in the 1950s and 1960s.

The Clinton administration is groping toward the invention of a "new" new capitalism. This "new" new model accepts the central tenet of Rooseveltian capitalism, which is that effective capitalism requires a large government sector, but it shifts government spending to financing resource creation and the efficient delivery of those services for which fee-for-services mechanisms for the rationing of access and the recovery of costs are either not effective or carry unacceptable social costs.[14]

7. Essential Flaws of Capitalism

I have not addressed the questions of what are the flaws that made capitalism a failure in 1933 and again in these days, and whether these flaws are the result of attributes of capitalism which are its essential characteristics. One striking flaw of capitalism—which was identified by Marx and Keynes—is its inability to maintain a close approximation to full employment over extended periods of time. The abysmally low standards of living that now exist within even relatively successful capitalisms are largely side effects of the inability to attain and sustain such approximations to full employment.

Keynes imputed this failure to the fact that capitalism is not merely a market economy: it is also a financial system. A fundamental aspect of capitalism is that there are *two* sets of prices. One set consists of the prices of current output. The second set consists of the prices of assets, both the capital assets used by firms in production and the financial instruments that firms issue in order to gain control of the fixed and working capital they need (see Minsky 1975; 1986).

Full Employment and Economic Growth as an Objective of Economic Policy: Some Thoughts on the Limits of Capitalism (1994)

Current output prices carry profits and are the mechanism by which costs are recovered. In the abstract, these prices are keyed to the money wage rate. The prices of capital assets and financial instruments are present prices for future streams of incomes. The proximate determinants are determined in different sets of markets. As a result, they are capable of varying, and they do vary, with respect to one another. Markets do not constrain capital asset and current output prices to a constant ratio.

The financial instruments issued by firms are held by households and financial institutions, such as banks, pension and mutual funds, and insurance companies.[15] Ever since the corporation became the dominant form of business organization, the liabilities of firms include equity shares as well as debts. The equity shares and some debts of some companies are freely traded on public markets: the market value of these instruments depends upon publicly available information. In practice, the price level of assets in a capitalist economy is an index of the market price of shares and debts.[16]

The reforms of the financial system during the Roosevelt era made transparency the overriding principle for corporate management and the operation of markets where financial instruments are issued and traded. Information about the operations of corporations and of markets on which equity shares are traded was to be freely available.[17]

Other liabilities of corporations—debts to banks and private placements—do not depend upon publicly available information, but rather on negotiation and discovery. Such debts, which are not marketable, can be syndicated among institutions, such as banks, insurance companies, and pension funds, which are deemed to be knowledgeable about processing private information.

As a result of the security market reforms of the Roosevelt era the law caught up with the fact that modern capitalism is corporate capitalism.

Over the 40-plus months of the great contraction the price level of current output fell by 33 percent, whereas the price level of equities on the stock exchanges fell by 85 percent. If the ratio of the prices of old and new capital assets was greater than 1:1 before

1929, in 1933 the ratio of old to new was 1:4. In 1933 no one would order new investment output when the second-hand market for capital assets was full of bargains.

In standard economic theory, prices are the terms upon which alternative goods and services are available. As the theory is set up, all that really matters are relative prices. However, to producers in a capitalist economy output prices recapture wage and material costs and carry profits (gross capital income). These profits enable a firm to pay the interest and principal that is due on debts, and to provide funds for dividends and retained earnings.[18] Inasmuch as debts are almost always denominated in money, to producers nominal prices matter. In the markets where assets, financial and real, are traded, prices reflect present views about future money flows. The market value of a firm is a capitalization of its nominal profits and therefore it is stated in nominal terms.

In a progressive capitalist economy investment outputs are a part of current output. When investment outputs are completed they are assimilated to the stock of capital assets: the investing firm pays the investment producer for the investment good. This payment is made with internal funds (retained earnings), funds raised by the sale of equities, and funds raised by debts, either as borrowings from banks or as the receipts from the sale of bonds. At the moment of purchase the value of a particular investment output changes from being determined by the sale price to being determined by the present value of the future incomes that operating and otherwise using this asset is expected to generate.

In practice, in a modern rich capitalist economy corporations are the principal proximate recipients of capital income or gross profits. A capitalist economy can be viewed as a set of interrelated balance sheets and income statements. There are two ultimates in this formalization: firms, which own the capital stock of the economy; and households, which own the financial liabilities of other units as assets. Financial institutions stand between firms and households. Today, to a large extent, the liabilities (equities and debts) of firms are owned by financial intermediaries of one type or another and the assets of households are largely liabilities of financial intermediaries.

Full Employment and Economic Growth as an Objective of Economic Policy: Some Thoughts on the Limits of Capitalism (1994)

These intermediaries—banks, savings institutions, insurance companies, mutual funds, and pension funds, to identify the most prominent financial intermediaries—are self-seeking (profit-seeking) institutions. In a modern capitalist economy, maximizing behavior is not restricted to households and firms that own capital assets: the entire array of financial intermediaries seeks profits. Each profit-seeking financial intermediary has its own agenda; they are not charitable institutions.

Of these profit-seeking, private-agenda financial organizations, one set plays an exceptionally delicate role in capitalist economies. This set consists of the investment or merchant bankers who either as brokers—who bring buyers and sellers together—or dealers—who take financial liabilities into their own accounts—act as midwives to company startups and the financing of continuing operations.

Essentially, these operators have superior knowledge about their customers who need financing (those who have a need for funds) and their customers who need outlets in which money can be placed. They turn this private knowledge—of the conditions under which funds are desired and the conditions under which funds are available—to their own advantage, even as they perform the social function of selecting the investments that the economy makes.

These financial intermediaries are of critical importance in determining the values attached to capital assets as collected in firms. In a balance sheet the book value of the owner's interest in the firm is the difference between the sum of the values entered for capital and financial assets and the value of debts. Dividing the book value of the owner's equity by the number of outstanding shares yields the book value of a share. However, for the main companies in a large economy, there is a thick market for equity shares and this market value may be less than, equal to, or greater than book value. A main consideration in decisions to invest is that the market valuation of the capital assets needs to exceed the supply price of the investment output, with a margin of safety that allows for the riskiness of the project.

One consequence of the introduction of these layers of profit-seeking organizations in the markets which determine the value of financial instruments is that the value of financial instruments, and therefore the value imputed to capital assets, can and does vary independently of the cost of investment outputs. Furthermore, the extent to which internal funds are expected to be available to finance investment depends upon the excess of anticipated cash flows from operations over the amount needed to service liabilities that were issued to finance such acquisitions in the past.

Because the capitalization rate depends upon present views of the future and the value of the secure assets in portfolios, the ratio of market price of capital in firms to the market price of investment outputs can vary. The very structuring of the argument in terms of a demand for investment output that depends upon the capitalizing of future profits and the determination of the supply price of outputs as dependent upon labor costs of producing these outputs ensures that the supply and demand relations would not, in economist jargon, be homogeneous of degree zero in either money or in money wages. The result would also not be independent of the extent to which positions of market power are capitalized into the price level of capital assets. Thus,

(a) the capitalist technique of valuing outputs and valuing capital assets,
(b) the market determination of liability structures, and
(c) the possibility of sharp increases and decreases in the t price of capital assets and financial instruments

lead to system-determined increases and decreases in the price of assets relative to the price level of current output. This ratio feeds into the amount of investment financed, which in turn leads to the flow of current profits.[19]

Once current profits fall sufficiently, or the carrying costs of debts [increase] sufficiently, so that the cash flows earned by operations or from financial assets by highly indebted operations are insufficient to meet commitments on liabilities, then the pressure of the need to validate debts (and for depository institutions to meet withdrawals) leads to a proliferation of attempts *to make positions*

Full Employment and Economic Growth as an Objective of Economic Policy: Some Thoughts on the Limits of Capitalism (1994)

by selling out positions. The result can be a sharp fall in asset values. A downward spiral in which investment ceases and profits evaporate can occur: the end result of overindebtedness can be a great or a serious depression.

Although the obvious flaw in capitalism centers around its inability to maintain a close approximation to full employment, its deeper flaw centers around the way the financial system affects the prices of and demands for outputs and assets, so that from time to time debts and debt servicing rise relative to incomes and conditions conducive to financial crises are endogenously generated. Once such a crisis is triggered, a collapse of investment followed by a long-lasting depression accompanied by mass unemployment will take place, unless a combination of lender-of-last-resort interventions by the central bank, which sustain asset prices, and enlarged government deficits, which sustain profits, takes place.[20]

This financial flaw cannot be eradicated from any form of market capitalism in which liabilities exist that are prior commitments of the gross nominal profit flows of businesses. Reforms which constrain the possibility of using excessive debts for specified purposes were part of the new model capitalism of the 1930s. Many aspects of these constraints were rendered ineffective by institutional evolution by the 1980s. In particular, constraints upon the assets eligible for the portfolios of the savings and loan associations were relaxed. The result was a series of crises of financial institutions and corporate indebtedness. A big depression did not happen in the early 1990s because the government validated the debts of the financial institutions that became insolvent, and huge government deficits sustained profits.[21]

The new model capitalisms that emerged out of the Great Depression and the Second World War had much larger government sectors than the failed model of the 1920s. Central banks were no longer constrained by the gold standard: they were now expected to use their ability to affect the behavior of banks to sustain income and employment and contain any thrust of the economy to an accelerating inflation or a deep deflation. The ability of a country to float its currency was much greater and the responsibility for maintaining aggregate demand by government, and even by international cooperation, was acknowledged.

For much of the period in which the new interventionist model worked well, the sole governor of the international system was the United States' commitment to maintain its domestic economy at a relatively close approximation to full employment and its willingness to run a trade deficit. This power of the United States within the world economy has been eroded as it has become a smaller part of the world economy.

Capitalism failed in 1929 because of the flaw inherent in the two-price-system nature of capitalism. In the 1930s and after the Second World War capitalism was reconstructed with a much greater government sector, which in the United States was largely devoted to sustaining consumption and military spending. Private investment remained the major determinant of the increase in productive capacity, and the amount of private investment still rested upon the price level of capital assets being greater than the supply price of investment outputs. The flaw in capitalism—that overindebtedness can lead to a sharp decline in the ability to validate debts and therefore to a sharp fall in the value of capital assets as collected in firms—remained, even though the structure of assets and liabilities in the first two decades after the Second World War did not allow for a debt deflation to occur.

8. Recent History

The recent history of the United States is a history of thrusts toward a debt deflation that were contained by a combination of central bank intervention and massive government deficits. The contained depression of the early 1990s first led to a sharp fall in short-term interest rates and, with a lag, by a fall in longer-term interest rates. This fall in interest rates raised the present values of income streams: asset values increased. This rise has abated the turbulence in US financial markets.

The capitalism that failed over 1929–33 was a small-government, constrained-central-bank, essentially laissez-faire economy.

Full Employment and Economic Growth as an Objective of Economic Policy: Some Thoughts on the Limits of Capitalism (1994)

The capitalism that had a good run after the Second World War was a big-government, interventionist economy with central banks that were less constrained than during the interwar years.

The post–Second World War model of capitalism was so successful over the first 20-plus years after the war that some are given to calling that period a Golden Age. In truth, it was not a utopian Golden Age, for each of us can find fault with some details of the economy of the 1950s and 1960s. But that performance might very well be a practical best. On an absolute scale, the most recent 20-plus years after the Second World War have not been bad, but they suffer by comparison with the early postwar period. However, a clear path of deterioration is discernible over recent years, in part because of policies such as those which Reagan and Thatcher exemplify, in part because of the way in which protracted success led to an acceptance of commitments to pay which erode the margins of safety that make capitalist firms and financial institutions resilient.

The junk bond episodes and the commercial construction excesses are built into the way in which business people and bankers interact in a capitalist economy. Only capitalist economies in which the regulatory agencies have stronger and more sophisticated controls than those of the regulatory agencies in the United States can avoid the financial excesses that bring financially complex economies to the brink of collapse.

9. Dimensions of the Crisis in Policy

"Why are the welfare states of post–Second World War capitalist economies now in crisis?" is the [next] question. I can answer for the United States.

The Social Security system, which is the keystone of the welfare state in the United States, was never adjusted for the enormous increase in life expectancy over the past 60 years. If life expectancies now were as they were 60 years ago there would be no crisis in the Social Security part of the United States' welfare state. The solution to this is rather simple: increase the age at which people retire. However, this would increase the labor force. Therefore, there is a need to increase the number of available jobs.

Another problem of the welfare state in the United States is with what is there called "welfare." This system—Aid to Families with Dependent Children (AFDC)—provides cash and in-kind support (medical care, housing, and food subsidies) to families with children, if income from work or assets is not available to support the children. In practice, a significant part of the population that is welfare-dependent is seemingly locked into a pattern of dependency: women who were raised by recipients of AFDC have children who in turn are being raised by a woman on AFDC. This welfare problem is increasingly viewed as a disaster in terms of the well-being of the recipients. However, the alternative to welfare is work for the mother and child care for the children.

Welfare reform leads to a similar problem as Social Security reform. To have people who are now on welfare or on Social Security entering the labor force increases the demand for jobs. The problems of the welfare state in the United States stem from the inability to achieve and sustain tight full employment.

We now live in a world where less than 3 percent of the United States' labor force is in agriculture and where a decreasing percentage of workers can produce all the standard manufactured goods that the economy demands. There is a need to support more workers in the production of socially useful outputs that are not manufactured goods and where the costs may not be recoverable by any simple fee-for-services arrangement. In the United States, military spending, on both weapons and manpower, supported workers whose costs were not covered by incomes based upon fees for services. Taxes and government borrowing raised the funds for these expenditures. There is a need to replace the military use of available resources with other forms of resource use which, like military spending, do not depend for their funding upon fees for services.

There is one crisis in the American welfare state apparatus which is different in kind from those in Europe. During the Second World War the United States began job-related health care "insurance" and job-related supplements to Social Security in the form of defined benefit pensions that were liabilities of corporations. Many corporations also took responsibility for the health care of their

Full Employment and Economic Growth as an Objective of Economic Policy: Some Thoughts on the Limits of Capitalism (1994)

retired workers. These pensions were not funded until the 1970s, and even now many are only partially funded. These pensions typically are vested after quite a few years on the job and until recently were not portable: workers were tied to corporations which presumably had secure market positions in perpetuity.

Over the past several years a large number of the great corporations of the United States have had serious financial difficulties. Some have gone into bankruptcy and others have downsized dramatically. Firms have taken drastic steps to reduce not only their shop-floor workers but also their overheads. Security of employment in the United States was never as great as in Japan, but it certainly was much greater in the past than it is today.

The newly revealed vulnerability of corporations means that the private-pension and health-care systems of the postwar period are no longer viable. The Clinton administration is attacking the problems of our health-care system. As yet there is no serious attack on the problems of the pension system that supplements Social Security.

The Clinton administration is a repudiation of the economics and social policies of the Reagan–Bush years. It accepts that there are government functions which are legacies of the past which need to be reconsidered. It denies the conservative assertion about the incompetence of government. The administration also recognizes that programs such as welfare, Social Security, and health care require reformulation.

A big issue as yet not addressed is how the United States is going to administer the industrial policy, which up to now has been carried in the military budget. The United States still has an unrivaled resource in the depth and wide distribution of research universities: almost every state has one or more, usually quite serious, establishments. Many of these state universities have strong applied-research interests, usually in fields that are closely related to the state's economy. The harnessing of the power to create and invent that such universities have, and the transformation of the development arms of the Defense Department into a civilian advanced-project agency, are frontiers that the Clinton administration will have to address as they fully develop an industrial policy.

The end result of the Clinton administration is likely to be a "new" new model capitalism that uses the model put in place in the 1930s as its point of departure. This "new" new model will not repudiate or attempt to dismantle the old new model, which was the aim of Reagan. The "new" new model of capitalism will explicitly recognize that the achievement of a full employment economy must come from organizations that are neither typical private corporations nor government departments, as we have understood them in the United States.

Initially, the corporation was a private organization chartered by a special act to carry out a public function. We can expect the "new" new model capitalism to create corporations which mix private and public funding to carry out programs that have social purposes. We can see glimpses of this in ideas that are being floated for health maintenance organizations, for the development of technologies, and for community development banking. It is not a matter of picking winners in some technological struggle, but rather a matter of defining needs that can be filled with known techniques but which require special organizations to carry them out.

There may well be some experimentation in taxation. The progressive income tax was compromised by Reagan.[22] The argument that consumption is a fairer basis for taxation than income is gaining some following. It is doubtful whether the political courage exists to recognize that the logic of a consumption tax requires that the fair rental value of owner-occupied housing should be entered into the consumption measure used for calculating the tax. However, a thorough and logical consumption-based tax system would simultaneously reintroduce meaningful progression into the tax system and cut through the confusions relating to capital gains and pension schemes.

As was mentioned earlier, pensions are a policy problem, due to the American system of a government Social Security system supplemented by private pension schemes, which in turn are publicly supported by the exemption from taxation of income placed in pension funds, either at the corporate level or at the beneficiary level.[23]

Full Employment and Economic Growth as an Objective of Economic Policy: Some Thoughts on the Limits of Capitalism (1994)

Furthermore, the income earned by the assets held by pension funds, as well as the portfolio gains, are exempt from taxes until the beneficiary begins to receive a pension from the fund.

10. Conclusion

In a tentative way the Clinton administration is trying to discover the contours of a "new" new model of capitalism: as yet it is not a conscious quest. But as one item in the menu of unmet needs leads to yet another, and as the administration seeks to define "the better" the country deserves, a "new" new model of capitalism will emerge which has as its anchors a commitment to full employment and a partnership of public and private agencies in the development of resources. This "new" new model will be based upon a more explicit recognition than anything that has hitherto guided policy in the United States: that the capitalist market technique of creating resources is flawed in that it is inherently myopic and needs to be permanently supplemented by the long view that government alone can have. Furthermore, in the complex system of product, labor, and financial markets that is a capitalist economy, the market mechanisms cannot achieve and maintain full employment. Institutions which supplement private employment with an open-ended supply of jobs are needed for capitalism to be successful.

Capitalism succeeded because it is a system that can take many forms, whereas the Soviet model of communism was unable to change its forms. Once a "new" new model of capitalism that is successful is put in place, we can be sure that the success will be transitory. For any model of capitalism that succeeds for a time will have features that constrain short-sighted myopic behavior which is to the apparent benefit of some economic agents. As a result, the efficacy of a particular structure of institutions and usages to bring about a successful economy will diminish.

Long ago Abba Lerner summed up the view put here as arguing that success brings into play market developments that breed failure. The problem of discovering and putting in place the institutions of a successful capitalism cannot be solved once and for all. Success is transitory. Future generations will have to confront a later version of the problem we now face: to turn a failing capitalism into a successful capitalism.

Notes

1. This is a quite broad reworking of a paper I presented in Milan, March 18–20, 1993, at a conference on "The Structure of Capitalism and the Firm in Contemporary Society." The call for that conference read: "When the whole world, so to speak, is capitalist it is timely and useful to question the limits of capitalism, its ability to provide answers to new contemporary problems, and the scope for intellectual innovations capable, to some degree at least, of remedying such limitations."

2. Roosevelt was inaugurated on March 4, 1933. Hitler had taken power on January 20, 1933. Newspapers like the Hearst press (which supported Roosevelt in the campaign of 1932) found much to praise in Mussolini's Fascism. Anti-laissez-faire ideas, such as President Theodore Roosevelt's New Nationalism, which looked to some form of state capitalism as a means of resolving problems of cyclical instability, insider manipulation of the financial system, growing importance of oligopoly, and the obvious inequality of income distribution, were very much "in the air." The Hoover administration had put in place, although they did not do much with it, the Reconstruction Finance Corporation, a government investment bank, which was a key organization in the Franklin Roosevelt variety of state capitalism. Several government financing organizations that still exist, such as the Home Loan Banks and the Export Import Bank, were spinoffs from the RFC.

3. Debt deflation is the label that Irving Fisher attached to the interactive process among debts, output prices, business cash flows, asset prices, and employment which took place over 1929–33 and other great depressions. See Fisher (1933) and Minsky (1982).

4. But, using a concept attributed to Yogi Berra, the Fat Lady has yet to sing: we may be in the midst of a debt deflation that is being played out on a longer time scale.

   The National Bureau of Economic Research tells us that an expansion began in late 1992. At the time of this writing (late 1993), the data indicate that the expansion is "a sometimes thing": the expansion has been moderate, another dip is possible, and the prospects for another set of crises in global financial markets are still alive.

   A period of 42 months elapsed between the stock market crash in 1929 and the bank holiday of 1933. If the much larger share of government in GNP and the financial system interventions—by which governments prevent the negative net worth of banks, savings institutions, and insurance companies passing through to the deposits and other nonequity liabilities—slow the debt deflation process, then a debt deflation process in today's institutional environment may take much longer to develop fully than the 42 months between October 1929 and March 1933. If we take the stock market crash of late 1987 as a triggering event for a possible debt deflation, then the repercussions of this stock market crash may not be fully played out.

Full Employment and Economic Growth as an Objective of Economic Policy: Some Thoughts on the Limits of Capitalism (1994)

One aspect of the Great Depression was that the economy stagnated for many months after the downside movement was contained. The current performance of the rich capitalist economies resembles that of stagnant economies.

5. The road to full employment would be easier if a concerted effort to achieve and sustain full employment was undertaken by the club of rich countries than if the United States took this path on its own. The United States' full-employment GNP may well be 10 percent greater than current measured GNP and at full-employment incomes the United States' huge trade deficit might well be substantially greater than at present. An across-the-board tariff of some 10 percent to 15 percent would constrain some of the leakage into imports of the stimulus from a full-employment policy and would be a good thing in its own right as a revenue measure.

6. In The New Dealers, Jordan A. Schwartz (1993) argues that the New Deal was largely an exercise in state capitalism, in which the government partook in the creation of financing vehicles for households and private business, the production of infrastructure, and the emergence of innovative productions. In Schwartz's view, much of the government's role in resource creation and the funding of innovation was transferred to the military in the era of hot and cold wars. The current need to develop a post–Cold War institutional structure which facilitates resource creation and facilitates the adoption of innovative products and processes is one way in which the Clinton and the New Deal eras resonate.

7. Little in the way of entitlements existed; I don't even know if the word had been coined. Two premises—no one will starve in America, and a dole is anathema—led to the "made work" programs of [the] WPA, CCC, and NYA.

8. In the early post–Second World War era buoyant private investment demand and the sustained level of military spending, combined with demand for housing, led to a close approximation to full employment being achieved, even as the ratio of government debt to GNP fell.

9. The Social Security system was not a large payout factor in the economy until the late 1960s and early 1970s, when retired workers with 30 and 35 years of employment under Social Security became common.

10. In the discussion of the Great Depression in the United States the focus is usually upon the unemployment rate and the fall in output prices. The fall in the indices of equity and of real-estate prices was much greater than the fall in GDP or in output prices as measured by the CPI.

    Arthur Miller's play The Price examines the effects through three generations on one family of the fall in the stock market. It is an excellent evocation of the emotional impact of the Great Depression on the previously well-to-do.

11. Michal Kalecki (1971). The Jerome Levy argument anent the relation between investment and profits is most accessible in Levy and Levy (1983). See also Minsky (1986).

12. Ronnie J. Phillips (1992) details the discussion of banking and financial system reform in the aftermath of the collapse of the financial system over 1929–33.

13. The immediate resolution of the banking crisis of 1933 was led by the Reconstruction Finance Corporation, which took equity positions in about 50 percent of the banks that reopened after the bank holiday. The Federal Reserve, which had been created in an effort to control systemic bank failures by supplying

liquidity, failed to stem systemic bank failures in the 1930s, when the problem was caused by the erosion of equity due to nonperforming assets.

In the savings and commercial bank crisis of the 1980s the Federal Reserve once again was unable to contain the failures and assure the validation of deposit liabilities: the Congress and the Treasury supplied the funds which validated deposits and contained the forced sale of assets. The Federal Reserve is not capable of containing a solvency crisis. A government investment bank / holding company is necessary if adverse system-wide consequences of an epidemic of nonperforming assets are to be contained.

14. A health care delivery system which guarantees universal access to some acceptable minimum of care is one major system that is part of a "new" new capitalism.

15. In a modern economy, household and government debts exist and are held by financial institutions and directly by households. These other liabilities both complicate the cash flows and offer routes which can either dampen [or] amplify the effect of the business and financial debt structure on the performance of the economy. In particular, whereas in a clean (no household debts, no government debts) economy, interest income is always a distribution of gross capital income, in our (in fact) dirty complex economy, interest income is also a distribution of wage incomes and a claim on tax revenues.

16. In principle, an index of the market price of existing capital assets is the appropriate index of asset prices to use in conjunction with the index of current output prices, but the information for such an index is not available. The growth of the holding company form of corporate capitalism means that entire lines of business are sold and bought. The model of the second price level needs to incorporate how the prices of such operating businesses are determined.

17. This freely available information means nothing unless sophisticated and knowledgeable analyses of this data exist. An effective transparent financial system requires security analysts, who distribute their analyses either for a fee or in exchange for the use of the services of their "firms." The lack of assurance about the integrity of security analysts may be an explanation for the rise of the open-ended mutual fund as the proximate supplier of equity and debt assets for households.

18. Retained earnings are the way the equity base of a corporation grows without recourse to the sale of equity on the public market.

19. The relation between the price level of capital assets and current output, along with other factors, determines the volume of aggregate demand and the excess or deficient demand for labor at the current wage rates. This excess or deficient demand will affect the movement of wages and thus the price level of investment output.

20. In this view, the intervention by a deposit insurance authority to ensure that deposits at "protected institutions" are paid at par is a central banking action.

21. This validation has been called a bailout.

22. The 1993 [Omnibus Budget Reconciliation Act] improved the fiscal picture, but it did not undo all the harm of the 1980s to the revenue system of the United States.

23. Whereas placements into pension accounts are to a limit (which is a substantial part of income for almost all) pretax dollars, employees' "contributions" to Social

Security are of aftertax dollars. Symmetry would call for making the "contributions" of employees to Social Security pretax dollars. Once this is done the reason for exempting social security payouts from taxation vanishes.

Sources

Fisher, I. 1933. "The Debt Deflation Theory of Great Depressions." *Econometrica* 1(4): 337–57.

Kalecki, M. 1971. ["The Determinants of Profits." Chap. 7 in] *Selected Essays on the Dynamics of a Capitalist Economy (1933-70)*. Cambridge, U.K.: Cambridge University Press.

Levy, S. J., and D. Levy. 1983. *Profits and the Future of the American Society*. New York: Harper & Row.

——. 1992. *How to Restore Long-Term Prosperity in the United States and Overcome the Contained Depression of the 1990s*. Special Report. Annandale-on-Hudson, N.Y.: Levy Economics Institute.

Minsky, H. P. 1982. "Debt Deflation Processes in Today's Institutional Environment." *Banca Nazionale del Lavoro Quarterly Review* 143 (December): 375–93.

——. 1975. *John Maynard Keynes*. New York: Columbia University Press.

——. 1986. *Stabilizing an Unstable Economy*. New Haven: Yale University Press.

Phillips, R. J. 1992. "The 'Chicago Plan' and New Deal Banking Reform." Working Paper No. 76. Annandale-on-Hudson, N.Y.: Levy Economics Institute. June.

Schwartz, J. A. 1993. *The New Dealers*. New York: Alfred A. Knopf.

Index

Aggregate demand, v, xi, xiv, 2, 8, 10–12, 14, 17, 23, 28, 37, 39, 69–71, 92, 93, 96, 97, 99, 106, 172, 180

Balance of payments, xix, 11, 12, 17, 18, 86, 94

Banks, 12, 122, 130, 133, 134, 147, 161–163, 167–169, 171, 173, 176, 178–180

Baumol, William, 44, 45, 54–59, 78

Business cycles, 92, 105, 110, 121, 134, 135, 164

Capitalism, iii, vii, viii, xiii, xx, 1, 32, 46, 71, 74, 75, 104, 110, 122, 123, 129, 130, 135, 146, 156, 157–162, 164–167, 171–173, 176–180

Capital shortage, 153–155

Choice theory, 111

Civilian Conservation Corps (CCC), iv, xvii, xx, 20, 150–152, 154, 159, 160, 179

Clinton, William Jefferson, vii, xix, 157, 158, 160, 166, 175–177, 179

Construction, 33, 34, 36, 64, 65, 67, 78, 142, 145, 146, 148, 149, 173

Consumption, xvi, xvii, 22, 85, 87, 90–93, 95, 97–101, 106–108, 111–118, 121, 165, 172, 176

Cooperatives, 155

Corporate structure, 147, 148, 155

Council of Economic Advisers (CEA), xii, xiii, xv, 2, 47

Debt, vii, xvi, 74, 120, 121, 130, 132, 141, 142, 145, 153, 159, 163, 165–172, 178, 180

Debt deflation, vii, 129, 135, 136, 142, 157, 164, 172, 178

Defense spending, 46, 69, 75, 104, 113, 115, 162, 165, 172, 174, 179

Deficit, budget, 162, 164, 165, 171, 172

Economic growth, xi, xiv, 15, 16, 27, 76, 114, 120, 141

Education, xi–xiv, xx, 15, 37, 57, 71, 77, 115

Employer of Last Resort (ELR), v, vi, xvii, xxi, 21–24, 39, 40, 77, 78, 149–153

Energy, 127, 148, 153, 154

Exchange rate, xix, 17, 92

Expectations, 30–32, 73, 87, 91, 99, 114, 119, 121, 122

Federal Reserve, 31, 107, 134, 135, 163, 164, 179, 180

Financial crisis, 122, 135, 164

Financial instability, v, vii, xxi, 30–32, 74, 75, 123, 129–135, 141

Financial reform, iii, vii, 159, 162

Financial structure, 109, 121, 129, 134, 159, 162–164

Financial system, vii, xvi, 74, 75, 109, 123, 129, 130, 134, 159, 163–171, 178–180

Fiscal policy, v, xii, xiii, 1, 11, 14, 15, 28, 31, 75, 86, 92, 107–109, 120, 122, 135

Fisher, Irving, 178

Food stamps, vi, 138–140, 152

Friedman, Milton, 69–71, 100, 107

Galbraith, John Kenneth, xii, 56, 105, 112

Gold standard, xx, 18, 162, 163, 171

Government spending, xvii, 15, 19, 31, 37, 48, 75, 108, 142, 150, 158, 159, 162, 165, 166

Great Depression, 4, 15, 47, 119, 122, 128, 134, 142, 162, 171, 178, 179

Great Society, 4, 18

Head Start, xii, 115

Housing, xvi, 100, 104, 127, 145–150, 162, 176, 179

Income distribution, v, viii, xvii, xviii, 9–12, 16, 17, 27–40, 43–45, 49, 58–60, 63, 67, 84, 92, 104, 109–120, 123, 135, 141, 159, 164, 165, 178

Inequality, xvi, xviii, 28, 29, 37, 68, 165, 178

Inflation, v, vi, xii, xvi, xviii, xix, xxi, 2, 10–13, 19, 31, 40, 45, 58, 69–71, 75, 85, 86, 91–95, 99, 100, 103, 107–109, 112, 115, 120, 122, 125, 127–129, 132, 134, 135, 138–141, 143–146, 149, 153, 158, 164, 171

Interest rates, 12, 74, 91, 94, 107, 165, 172

Investment boom, xvi, 28, 30–32, 69, 74, 92, 114, 132

Johnson, Lyndon B., iii–xvii, xx, 68, 103, 108, 115, 119, 150

Kaldor, Nicholas, 31, 80

Kennedy, John F., iii, xii–xiv, xvii, 68, 103, 108, 112, 114, 119, 121, 122, 150, 164, 165

Keynes, John Maynard, xiv, 44, 101, 105, 106, 110, 121, 123, 142, 166

Keynesian, xi, xiii–xv, 30, 68, 76, 101, 105–110, 119–121, 128, 142

Labor force participation, 8, 76, 77, 87, 88, 140, 141

Labor supply, 7, 13, 19, 71, 89, 91–93, 96–99

Laissez-faire, 135, 159, 160, 162, 166, 172, 178

Liquidity preference, 87, 91–94, 98, 99

Manufacturing, 33–36, 64–68, 143–146, 149

Marshall, Alfred, 110–112, 123

Marx, Karl, 110, 123, 166

McGovern, George, 103, 112, 116, 139

Migration, 36, 38, 40

Minimum wage, v, xv, 21–24, 39, 149, 150

Mini-panic, 31, 75

Monetary policy, 12, 14, 18, 94, 109, 121

Monopoly, 129, 146, 147

Nationalization, 148

National Youth Administration (NYA), iv, xvii, xx, 20, 151, 152, 154, 159, 179

Negative income tax, vi, 29, 30, 43, 46, 49, 51, 81–101, 112, 116, 139

Neoclassical, vi, 104–113, 116, 119–123

New Deal, iv, vii, viii, xvii, xx, 20, 142, 159, 160, 179

Nixon, Richard, 103, 107, 109, 112, 116, 128, 136, 150

Okun's law, xv, 6

Pareto, Vilfredo, 105, 106, 111

Pensions, xxi, 49, 174–176

Phillips curve, 12, 13, 25, 31, 69

Political barriers, vi, xix, 31, 45, 50, 51, 69

Portfolios, 95, 98, 119, 121, 122, 130, 163, 170, 171

Price stability, 92, 94, 96, 160, 188

Productivity, xviii, xix, 8–10, 38, 40, 54–56, 70, 71, 74, 79, 80, 106, 126, 141

Index

Profits, xvi, xix, 9, 10, 31, 40, 59, 80, 113–115, 118, 129, 132, 145, 148, 162, 164, 167–171, 179

Public employment, iv, xvii, xviii, 21, 24, 46, 49, 71–73

Public goods/services, 29, 44, 46, 49, 69, 73, 74, 77, 104, 109, 112, 114, 115

Public works, 20, 21, 160

Race, 11, 15, 38, 58, 59, 61–63, 70, 73, 115

Reagan, Ronald, 165, 166, 173, 175, 176

Recession, 32, 73–75, 109, 125, 135, 136, 142, 153, 164

Reconstruction Finance Corporation, 163, 178, 179

Redistribution, 46–54, 59, 77, 80, 118

Relative wages, 6, 7, 16, 28, 32–38, 40, 49, 54, 59, 61, 63–69, 73, 75, 76, 129, 142–146

Research and development, 15, 37

Retirement age, 140, 152

Roosevelt, Franklin D., 128, 157, 159–163, 165–167, 178

Rural poverty, 29, 36, 40

Samuelson, Paul, 25, 70

Savings, 30, 31, 76, 82, 153, 169, 171, 178, 180

Simons, Henry Calvert, 30, 100

Social dividend, vi, 43, 81–86, 100, 112

Social Security, iv, xxi, 22, 76, 86, 137, 138, 140, 152, 173–176, 179, 180

Solow, Robert, 25, 70

Speculation, 74, 91, 106, 119–122, 129, 130, 159

Structuralist, xii, xiv, xv, 13

Sweden, 5, 13, 20, 127, 154

Taxes, xxi, 9, 14, 43, 51, 59, 73, 77, 81–101, 108, 118, 138, 147–150, 174, 177

Thatcher, Margaret, 165, 166, 173

Tight full employment, iv–viii, xv–xxi, 2–4, 10–13, 16–18, 21, 23, 25, 27, 28, 32, 61, 68, 69, 76, 174

Tobin, James, 103, 112–114, 122

Training, xii, 1, 7, 19, 20, 23, 61, 115

Transfer payments, iv, 2, 3, 29, 30, 46, 49, 76, 97, 136–138, 140, 141, 149, 152, 159, 160, 164, 165

Trickle down, xviii, 15, 58, 69, 150, 156

Unions, 7, 10, 135, 142–145, 164

Urban poverty, 29, 40, 78, 151

Utilities, 104, 127, 148

Vietnam War, 58, 69, 75, 95, 113, 114, 128

Volcker, Paul, 166

Wage and price controls, 33, 149

Wallace, George, 58, 70, 115

Walras, Léon, 105–111, 120

War on Poverty, iii–vi, xi–xvi, xx, xxi, 2, 4, 11, 14, 20, 27, 63, 86, 115, 116

Welfare state, vi, 136–141, 159, 160, 173, 174

Works Progress Administration (WPA), iv, xvii, xx, 20, 23, 150–154, 159, 179

World War II, xiii, xiv, 4, 6, 13, 30, 32, 33, 38, 39, 65, 67, 95, 121, 134, 142, 143, 151, 155, 171–174

Biographies

Dimitri B. Papadimitriou is president of the Levy Economics Institute of Bard College, executive vice president and Jerome Levy Professor of Economics at Bard College, and managing director of ECLA of Bard, Berlin. His research includes financial structure reform, fiscal and monetary policy, community development banking, employment policy, and distribution of income, wealth, and well-being. He heads the Levy Institute's macroeconomic modeling team studying and simulating the US and world economies. In addition, he has authored or coauthored many articles in academic journals and Levy Institute publications relating to Federal Reserve policy, fiscal policy, financial structure and stability, employment growth, and Social Security reform. In 2008, he was instrumental in the republication of Hyman P. Minsky's seminal *Stabilizing an Unstable Economy* and *John Maynard Keynes* by McGraw-Hill.

Papadimitriou has testified on a number of occasions in hearings of Senate and House of Representatives Committees of the US Congress, was vice-chairman of the Trade Deficit Review Commission of the US Congress and was a member of the Competitiveness Policy Council's Subcouncil on Capital Allocation. He was a distinguished scholar at the Shanghai Academy of Social Sciences (PRC) in fall 2002. Papadimitriou has edited and contributed to 13 books published by Palgrave Macmillan, Edward Elgar, and McGraw-Hill, and is a member of the editorial boards of the *Journal of Economic Analysis*, *Challenge*, and the *Bulletin of Political Economy*. He is a graduate of Columbia University and received a Ph.D. in economics from the New School for Social Research.

L. Randall Wray is a senior scholar at the Levy Economics Institute of Bard College and a professor of economics at the University of Missouri–Kansas City. His current research focuses on providing a critique of orthodox monetary theory and policy, and the development of an alternative approach. He also publishes extensively in the areas of full employment policy and, more generally, fiscal policy. With President Dimitri B. Papadimitriou, he is working to publish, or republish, the work of the late financial economist Hyman P. Minsky, and is using Minsky's approach to analyze the current global financial crisis.

Wray is the author of *Money and Credit in Capitalist Economies*, 1990; *Understanding Modern Money: The Key to Full Employment and Price Stability*, 1998; and *Modern Money Theory: A Primer on Macroeconomics for Sovereign Monetary Systems*, 2012. He is also coeditor of, and a contributor to, *Money, Financial Instability, and Stabilization Policy*, 2006, and *Keynes for the 21st Century: The Continuing Relevance of The General Theory*, 2008.

Wray taught for more than a decade at the University of Denver and has been a visiting professor at Bard College, the University of Bologna, and the University of Rome (La Sapienza). He received a BA from the University of the Pacific and an MA and a Ph.D. from Washington University, where he was a student of Minsky.